AMERICAN PSYCHOLOGY SERIES

HENRY E. GARRETT, GENERAL EDITOR

AMERICAN PSYCHOLOGY SERIES

PSYCHOLOGICAL DIAGNOSIS IN SOCIAL ADJUSTMENT

By PERCIVAL M. SYMONDS
Teachers College, Columbia University

THE PSYCHOLOGY OF THE AUDIENCE

By H. L. HOLLINGWORTH
Barnard College, Columbia University

THE PSYCHOLOGY OF THE AUDIENCE

By

H. L. HOLLINGWORTH

Professor of Psychology
Barnard College, Columbia University

AMERICAN BOOK COMPANY

New York   Cincinnati   Chicago   Boston   Atlanta

"There be three things
Which are too wonderful for me,
Yea, four which I know not.

The way of an eagle in the air;
The way of a serpent upon a rock;
The way of a ship in the midst of the sea;
And the way of a man with a maid."

Proverbs XXX, 18

—

And if Agur, the son of Jakeh, had been
perfectly honest he would have added:
"Yea, even a fifth thing sometimes puzzles me,—
The way of a speaker with his audience."

PREFACE

This volume owes its existence first of all to the members of a college debating club, who invited the author to give them a lecture on the psychology of the audience. In complying with this request a search was made for such matter-of-fact and experimentally verified data as the literature of social psychology and of public speaking might afford. The search was but poorly rewarded. Rules and principles were found in sufficient number, and advice was freely offered in manuals; but little but personal opinion was offered in support of the various admonitions.

The appetite of the debating club was easily enough satisfied, but by that time an intrinsic interest in the topic had developed. Investigations were found the results of which seemed directly applicable to the psychology of the audience, however foreign this interest may have been to the original investigator. A few experimental studies dealing directly with audience situations were discovered. New ones were instituted by students and fellow workers. Gradually the results appeared to lend themselves to systematic presentation. They were meager and often inconclusive, but they led to further inquiries and made it possible to conduct a short seminar on the topic.

The topic was then laid by for maturation. But it soon proved to be a subject of interest to those outside the laboratory and the classroom. Teachers of public speaking, clergymen, extension institutes, and clubs asked to have the topic considered. The original one lecture expanded into several. The Christian Advocates then asked to be permitted to publish the material as an article, and this was done.

Organizations of speech specialists undertook on their own account several experimental studies in this field. Some of their members urged that, however incomplete the material, it be made available through publication as a survey of our present information. When a publisher, through one of his editors, desired to produce a book on the topic, the last defense broke down and the manuscript was released.

The author's hope is that, as an account of our more or less experimentally verifiable knowledge up to date, flavored with a mild touch of general psychological analysis, the survey may lead to more extended and more rapid advances in the study of a group of problems that have at once a genuine psychological interest and a widespread practical importance.

H. L. H.

CONTENTS

ix

CHAPTER I

INTRODUCTION

The psychology of the audience is an ancient theme, older certainly than the origin of language. Students of the coquetry and courtship of the lower animals have made much of the role of the audience in the antics of infra-human love making. And before the days of spoken language, vocal cries, gesture, facial expression, and overt conduct surely had their relation to the auditor and the spectator.

The craving for an audience represents one of humanity's fundamental needs. Without an audience women relapse and men become unkempt. Apathy with respect to the human environment is one of the grave signs of mental disorder. Except for the impulse of exhibitionism, the material, artistic, and spiritual achievements of men would surely have moved more slowly. One of the most significant things about an individual is the type of audience which more or less implicitly motivates his thought and conduct.

Explicit discussions of the audience are at least as old as the institution of oratory. Even the most recent expositions relating to the audience, and to the crowd or mob as well, have chief reference to the technique of oratorical appeal. And it is a matter of some interest that the spoken appeal has attracted more attention than has the written or printed record. In English the word "audience" serves at once to denote those collective phenomena that occur under the influence of the spoken word, as in the case of a congregation. But we have no similar word for the witnesses of a spectacle, or for the readers of an essay,—no word like "spectience," corresponding to the common collective word "audience." Movie, tableau, circus, painter, poet, all alike borrow the term "audience," though auditors they usually have none, in their respective arts.

We must therefore use the word "audience" throughout this book with the extended meaning commonly allowed to it. To have an audience will therefore mean not only to be heard, although this will be throughout the dominant or major meaning. But we shall also use the word to indicate in a general way the definitely social situation in which one individual is the object of attention on the part of other human beings. In this sense the acrobat, or the baseball player, or the pugilist has an audience. So also have the journalist, the poet, the portrait painter. Even the silent motion-picture actor has his or her audience, although it is only a secondary representation or picture that is actually witnessed; the radio broadcaster has an audience, although the sounds actually heard are really produced by the intervention of many different mechanisms.

We live always amongst a cloud of witnesses; these comprise our audience, in the general sense. The plays of children often languish or notably change in form when the audience departs. The adolescent youth is often so conscious of the presence of spectators that he painfully parades before them, or perhaps is handicapped by the consequent personal attention he must bestow on his every act. "Thou, God, seest me," or some equivalent conception, may constrain the conduct of the mature. The loss of an accustomed audience may spell mental or moral disaster in the unstable. In the old it adds to the sense of individual futility. Retired preachers often continue writing sermons in their dotage, and may even insist on reading them to the members of the family, or on issuing them in booklets.

It was the "audience" in this extended meaning that William James had in mind when he wrote so confidently of "A man's social self" which is "the recognition which he gets from his mates." The paragraph [30] * is worth quoting by way of emphasizing the need for an audience, which is a common trait of the human being.

"We are not only gregarious animals, liking to be in sight of our fellows, but we have an innate propensity to get ourselves noticed, and noticed favorably, by our kind. No more fiendish punishment could be devised, were such a thing physically possible, than that one should be turned loose in society and remain absolutely unnoticed by all the members thereof.

"If no one turned round when we entered, answered when we spoke, or minded what we did, but if every person we met 'cut us dead,' and acted as if we were nonexisting things, a kind of rage and impotent despair would ere long well up in us, from which the cruelest bodily tortures would be a relief; for these would make us feel that, however bad might be our plight, we had not sunk to such a depth as to be unworthy of attention at all."

One of the most interesting things about the psychology of the audience is the striking conflict, so often present, between the need or craving for an audience, and the fear of it. Scarcely less universal than the demand for an audience is the distressing experience known as "stage fright." One of our chief concerns must be with this profound effect, and other quite diverse effects, of

* All references are made by number, the numbers being those found in the bibliography at the end of the book.

the audience upon the performer. But first we must consider the larger amount of available material dealing with the effect of the performer upon the audience.

Up to the present time practically all of the discussions concerned with the audience have had to do chiefly with the "art" of manipulation. Their motivation has been that of increasing the speaker's practical effectiveness, or of exhibiting or illustrating the technique of the orator. Little effort has been made to bring together in scientific expression such principles as may underlie the mutual reactions of speaker and audience. Almost no effort has been made actually to measure the presumed influences of this or of that bit of technique. The experimental approach, in other words, has scarcely been attempted.

In recent years the nature of the typical "audience" has undergone radical modification. For one thing the diffusion of learning has produced audiences of unprecedented sophistication. Furthermore, the varied mechanical means of facilitating communication and of extending its area have resulted in the production of audiences of enormous magnitude, and of fluctuating audiences that cover long stretches of time and that repeatedly face the same presentation or a mechanically perfect duplication of it. The printing press, the phonograph, the motion picture, the radio will serve to suggest the numerous changes, so profound and far reaching that what was once a private recital or a mere oration now readily becomes a piece of national propaganda or an instrument of wholesale education or recreation.

It seems worth while at such a time to attempt to bring together such bits of experimental material as have slowly accumulated and to state as well as may be what scientific principles can be formulated with respect to the psychology of the audience. The limitations of such an enterprise will be set by the fund of knowledge available, and this is small. The present volume undertakes in the main to give a brief account within these limits.

The writer has been directly associated with but a few of the investigations and experiments which are herein reported. His chief task has been the assembly and organization of results which have hitherto appeared only in widely scattered places. Often, indeed, no recognition has before been given to the bearing of these results on the psychology of the audience, and here the task has been not only that of discovering the reports but also of indicating their applications to the present topic. Our debt is great, then, to the authors of these original studies, to whom due credit will be given in connection with the discussion of the results of each. It is hoped that the value and influence of each of these scattered studies will be increased by their assembly and organization around a single theme. In the bibliography at the end of the book full references are given to those whose results have been useful in the preparation of this volume.

USEFUL CONCLUSIONS AND PRACTICAL SUGGESTIONS

1. The passion for an audience is one of humanity's fundamental cravings.

2. Apathy with respect to the social environment or audience is likely to be a sign of mental peculiarity and often of grave disorder.

3. One of the most significant things about a person is the type of audience that motivates and determines his thought and conduct.

4. The word audience serves to denote not only groups of listeners but also groups of spectators, readers, and observers of all kinds.

5. The reaction of one's audience is a strong force in spurring activity in every kind of achievement, even that accomplished in solitude.

6. There could be no punishment more disturbing than being completely ignored by one's audience, in the larger social sense.

7. The modern audience is sophisticated to an unprecedented degree, and modern techniques make possible enlarged audiences, far exceeding the scope of primitive face-to-face groups.

CHAPTER II

PRELIMINARY ANALYSIS

It has been said that only those who are deficient in the sense of humor ever undertake to write a scientific treatise on the comic. They do this, it is said, only to have a theoretical explanation of why other people laugh when they themselves do not. Essays on "How to Succeed" are seldom written by those who have had the experience. It must be confessed also that to discuss the winning of an audience need not constitute a pretense to the possession of that skill. But oratory, even as courtship, is at least a two-sided affair. We have all been members of audiences, and in that status we have had much experience in being lost or won by the speaker or other performer. Who, after all, has a better right to discuss the psychology of the audience than the audience itself?

We may agree, to begin with, that many human reactions occur without being clearly understood. The performer may effectively win his audience without deliberate knowledge of the technique he employs. The audience, on the other hand, may react favorably or unfavorably without being able to analyze the motives or stimuli to its behavior. Anecdotes of success or failure, arbitrary rules, and rostrum conventions may attempt to convey the actual processes involved in such situations; or blind imitation may seek to reproduce the result. These methods we shall leave, in the main, to the teacher of public speaking, our own enterprise, instead, taking the form of an attempt to analyze the problem into its elements, with emphasis on the elements of science rather than on the details of art in the successful performer-audience relation.

Comparative reading of the specialists who have written advice on public speaking suggests that even in the case of the conscious elements there is contradiction among experts, and few universal rules exist. Thus Kleiser [37] instructs his readers that a speaker "should look his audience squarely in the eye, as this is one of the most effective means of riveting attention." On the other hand, Bautain [4] declares:

"For the greatest possible avoidance of distractions I will recommend a thing which I have always found successful; that is, not to contemplate the individuals who compose the audience and thus not to establish a special understanding with any one of them. . . . As for myself I carefully avoid all ocular contact with no matter whom, and I restrict myself to a contemplation of the audience as a whole,—keeping my looks above the level of the heads."

And again, just as definitely, McIlvaine [45] insists:

"The speaker's eye should be fixed upon the audience. It is indispensable that the speaker should not allow his eye to become fixed upon the manuscript, nor to wander around the walls. . . . He must bring his eye to bear steadily upon the people before him, scanning their countenances individually, and noting every sign of attention or the want of it."

THE TASK OF ANALYSIS

We may be sure that the enumeration of artifices and devices is at least the wrong way to begin the study of winning an audience. For our present purpose, we shall scarcely consider the mechanics of speech, the canons of expression, form, inflection, and gesture, leaving these in the main to the voice specialist. And we shall leave to the rhetorician the consideration of the literary details of form and finish, force and emphasis, organization and sequence. Moreover, we must, for the most part, leave to the logician the study of evidence and the nature of proof and fallacy.

Furthermore, for our purpose, we must abstract, from the varied concrete sorts of audiences and purposes of congregation, only those features more or less common to them all. Audiences assemble from a variety of motives,—to be entertained, instructed, exhorted; to observe merely, to participate, to dominate. Their occasions, places, and modes of assembly are equally diverse, —street corner, theater, church, stadium, circus tent, college hall, parliamentary chamber, banquet table, smoking room. No less varied are the functions of the performer. Dancing, singing, talking, fighting, juggling, parading, praying,—these are only samples of the long list of functions performed before audiences.

Each of these situations has no doubt its own psychology. Processes and acts peculiar to each set of circumstances will be of great importance to the performer, of vital concern to the audience, and of scientific interest to the mere observer. The special characteristics of most occasions, topics, places, and motives may, indeed, be the factors most determinative of the success or failure of the performer-audience relation.

We must, however, concern ourselves here with such features as are in the main common to all or to several of these situations. The available material, it must be said, is most closely related to the spoken performance, and to the passive audience, assembled for purposes of aural entertainment, instruction, or exhortation, or, in part for deliberation. The restrictions imposed upon such a discussion are obvious. Similar restrictions would be encountered in a book dealing with "gardening" in general, rather than with the special nurture and idiosyncrasies of particular flowers or vegetables. But the general treatise on gardening has its own proper place, along with the special handbook on asparagus or strawberries. In a similar way the general consideration of audience phenomena is worth undertaking, even though it be compelled to abstract from the specific and concrete details which any particular audience situation may involve.

To begin with, moreover, there are some performers who, by virtue of their particular personal appeals, their appearance, voice, history, or through other associations which may attach to them, win us from the start, without the use of any special technique and in spite of generally unfavorable setting or circumstances. Magnificent stage presence, such as that of Bryan or Münsterberg, is more a matter of nature than of nurture and device. It is however true that picturesque associations and eccentricities of garb or bearing, as in the case of "Buffalo Bill" Cody, or "Billy" Sunday, may go far to compensate for a native appeal otherwise inadequate. Lindbergh, the "lone eagle of the sky," interests an audience from the start, because of the intrinsic thrill of his own earlier acts. A presidential candidate, a "favorite son," or a member of a royal family draws and holds an audience, regardless of his personal effectiveness, through the glamour of political party or other excitement.

It would be to no purpose to catalogue these fortunate details of personality or experience, and little is possible in the way of an exact psychology of such advantages. Few of us possess them, and the attempt to cultivate them artificially will meet with dubious success. They are as varied and as numerous as are the individuals and the episodes of life. Some indication of their variety and subtlety is given in the following statement from an earlier investigator, C. H. Woolbert, in a monograph written in 1916.

"The speaker begins to carry meaning from the moment he appears. First, his personal appearance affects those before him. If he is tall and straight, his influence is different from that of the speaker short and bent; if he is rotund, he impresses men one way; if slender, in another; the man with a Jovian brow and an Apollo-like carriage means a thing quite different from the man whose head is small and who stands like a frightened fawn.

"Then his clothes also mean much; the well-groomed man means one thing to an audience; the unkempt, unbrushed man means something quite different. The manner of dressing the hair, even the possession or lack of hair, the way of looking at the audience, the speaker's stride, his manner of taking his seat, of switching his coat-tails, of using his handkerchief,— all these visually apprehended details have a significance for the observer. . . . Once his voice disturbs the hearer's ears with sound waves, the auditors begin to place new estimates upon the object before them."

Each detail of the performer's appearance, personality, reputation, and conduct contributes toward such effects, in a positive or a negative way. Important as they are in practice, these are not, however, the influences that are most to concern us. Instead of these multifarious aids or handicaps, we are chiefly to consider in this book the more impersonal and general features which characterize the relation of any performer to the relatively few types of audiences.

THE SPEAKER AND THE ADVERTISEMENT

No disparagement is implied in drawing an analogy between the usual speaker or performer and the common printed instrument of business publicity. As a matter of fact, the winning of an audience is in many ways like the task accomplished by the successful advertisement. It differs from the problem of conducting a personal conversation in much the same way that the task of the printed advertisement differs from that of the oral salesman. The salesman, working at close range and face to face with his prospect or customer, may choose his appeal, vary it, repeat it, or supplement it according to the immediate time and place or circumstance. The advertisement, on the other hand, in addition to other frailties, must from the nature of its work be addressed not to a single individual nor in general even to individuals of the same type and interest. It must address itself, within certain limits, to the average individual or standard person of a group,—an individual who, as thus defined, has no concrete existence. In the same way the speaker or other public performer must meet the audience as a whole, not merely selected members of it. Analogy with the advertisement affords at least a neat starting point for analysis of the psychology of the relation of the performer to his audience.[24]

THE FIVE FUNDAMENTAL TASKS

Analysis shows that there are five tasks which the complete advertisement undertakes,—namely, to Catch, Hold, Impress, Convince, and Direct the prospect. The reader's ATTENTION must be caught; that is, diverted from its present object to the general field or space occupied by the appeal. His INTEREST must be held long enough for the appeal to impress his MEMORY with the significant details. These details must carry sufficient CONVICTION or PERSUASION so that the reader will be led to some specific ACTION to which the appeal directs him. He writes for information, purchases, recommends, or makes a memorandum.

But not all advertisements attempt all five of these tasks. Only the *complete* appeal is so ambitious. The *publicity* appeal undertakes the first three tasks, leaving the remaining two to be accomplished in other ways. The *classified* appeal assumes the first two tasks as already accomplished, and the third as able to take care of itself; it directs itself only to the last two of the five tasks. Each variety is "winning the reader," but the different types begin or cease operation at different points in the process.

Now the task of winning an audience, as undertaken by the speaker, is also complex and involves much the same array of tasks. But in a given case the process begins or ceases at a particular point, and only in certain instances does it involve the whole series of tasks. Where it begins and where it ends depend in part, of course, on the purpose of the speaker, but most of all on the types of audience. The speaker is chosen for a given occasion, and it is the presence and the type of the audience that constitutes the occasion.

Consideration of the numerous occasions for assembly, other than that of listening to a speaker, will show clearly that these five primary tasks are not all involved in every audience situation. The antics of children and the parading of Easter garments are, in the main, directed to an audience. But here the mere attracting of attention suffices, since prolonged interest, memory, persuasion, and specific action touch no part of the exhibitionist craving.

The vaudeville performance, the circus, the concert, and the motion picture, however, endeavor to go one step further. They seek, that is, not only to attract initial attention but also to hold interest. Retention, conviction, and decision, however, are beyond their usual aim. The ordinary schoolroom affords a familiar example of the inclusion of the third task,—that of effecting permanent retention. Any deliberative assembly, as a committee meeting, a caucus, a session of the legislature, shows the inclusion of the fourth task, that of persuasion or conviction. If votes are to be cast, policies determined, wares sold, or deeds of violence committed, then the fifth task, involving specific and overt action, comes clearly into consideration.

Audience situations differ not only in the ultimate task which they involve. They differ also, as we shall see in another connection, in the point or task at which action begins. Any audience situation may thus be described from three points of view,—the number of the primary tasks involved, the task which the situation prescribes as the initial point of action, and the ultimate task, at which point the audience situation dissolves.

For general purposes, as well as for practical ones, the mere number of tasks seems relatively unimportant as a basis for the classification of audiences. That such a classification is feasible, however, the foregoing examples have sought to show. They have at the same time illustrated the mode of classification of audiences based on the point or task at which the audience situation dissolves. Since the preliminary tasks appear to be much the same, however far in the series of tasks the performer is required to go, such a classification is perhaps of little instructiveness. More important is a classification based on the point or task at which the performer's activity is supposed to begin. Upon such considerations the performer must base his preparation and further conduct; upon the accuracy of his diagnosis of the state of preparedness of his audience his ultimate as well as his immediate success will depend. In our later analysis, therefore, we shall seek to describe audiences and classify them in terms of the point in the series of five tasks at which the performer is expected to begin.

THE COLLECTIVE ASPECT OF AUDITORS

No little psychological interest attaches to the absence from our language of a collective noun to designate a congregation of spectators. For those who see we have only the plural forms of singular nouns,—"witnesses," "spectators," "observers," corresponding to the "listeners," "auditors," and "hearers" of the spoken presentation. But in the latter case we have in addition the collective singular name "audience." No corresponding term, such as "spectience," is in use, and presumably the need for it has not been felt.* This suggests the early and continued recognition that the auditory appeal is able in some special way to weld the multitude of auditors into an effective unit. The auditors become one, the spectators remain many.

It is unnecessary to suppose that, in the case of auditors, any super-individual mind or group consciousness is involved. The simple fact is that auditors, it would seem, are more likely to act in concerted fashion than is the case with spectators. Two reasons for this difference may be suggested.

In the first place, the auditory appeal pursues each

---

* On the other hand, we have no word specifically related to "hearing" in the way that reading is related to "seeing." "Understanding" is available, but it applies equally to what is seen and to what is heard.

member of the congregation, more or less regardless of his bodily attitudes and adjustments. The ear hears, whether or not it be directed toward the spatial source of the sound. And the appeal is practically uninterrupted, since the ear cannot be closed as can the eye. Hence at every instant the auditors are quite likely to be assailed by the same features of the appeal, and the conditions are more favorable for concerted response, which, when it appears, will suggest unitary reaction.

In the second place, the appearance of unitary response is in part due to the sympathetic suggestion exerted by each member of the group upon his neighbors. Signs of emotion, of interest and enthusiasm, or approval or resentment, of apathy or protest, of amusement, sorrow, or tenderness, on the part of a neighbor, tend reflexly to arouse similar feelings or attitudes in the observer. These signs are more likely to consist of facial changes, bodily attitudes, gestures, and other visible manifestations, than of clues that can be heard. In the case of the spectacle, attention to the appeal interferes with the observation of these expressive reactions in one's neighbors, inasmuch as visual attention involves direct fixation of the eye upon the object of regard, and peripheral or marginal vision is vague in detail and lacks vividness. Attention at best can in such circumstances only fluctuate roughly from one to the other.

But in the case of the auditory appeal, the main stimulus, the presentation, may be followed while the eye meanwhile and concurrently takes note of the neighboring signs of emotion and attitude. Appeal of speaker and appeal of neighbor focus upon a single point and moment. A general *rapport* is thus established or at least possible of establishment. It is this that underlies the concerted responses of the audience, as distinguished from the many separate orientations of a group of spectators.

All that is required to exhibit the fact of this influence of the focused appeals is the separation of the auditors so as to exclude the visual observation of one another. This is effectually accomplished in the case of the auditors of a broadcast radio presentation. The situation now more closely resembles that of the group of spectators. The feeling of strangeness reported by the performer in his earlier broadcasting experience is in part due to the realization of this fact. It is of course also due in part to the feeling of remoteness, the visual absence of the presumed auditors, and the lack of indications of direction or degree of interest which the ordinary audience affords through its applause, its restlessness, and similar signs.

And on the other hand the reaction of the auditors is found to differ when the auditory appeal is reinforced by the appearance, gesture, and facial expression of the performer. Such dissociation of stimuli often plays havoc with the rumored reputation of an orator. The radio appeal falls flat or repels, showing how much of the face-to-face effectiveness was due not to spoken sounds but to visual appearance, gesture, and other bodily activity.

PRACTICAL CONCLUSIONS

1. The members of an audience are likely to be as good judges of its psychology as is the performer who appears before it.

2. An audience may react favorably or unfavorably without knowing the nature of the factors or stimuli that govern its actions.

3. A public performer may be successful without realizing the basis of his success.

4. Dogmatic rules and arbitrary devices do not always work as predicted by the experts, who themselves disagree in many of their recommendations.

5. An artifice or device that succeeds with one performer or one audience may fail on other occasions, and it is safest to distrust such methods.

6. Every audience and every performer has a special psychology, but there is also a general psychology of the performer-audience relation, which we here seek to formulate.

7. Every performer, by virtue of features, bearing, voice, associations, and reputation exerts a definite psychological effect the moment he appears before the audience.

8. The technique of influencing an audience follows the same general plan as that of the successful printed appeal, such as an advertisement or a poster.

9. The successful performance may involve any or all of the five fundamental tasks or steps, which are Attention, Interest, Impression, Conviction, and Direction.

10. Audience situations differ in the step at which the performer begins and in the number of ensuing steps that are to be undertaken.

11. This series of steps is not a mere sequence of stages, but the tasks overlap and the performance is often a complex and cumulative process.

12. An appeal to hearing has the advantage of pursuing each member of the audience regardless of his own bodily attitude and posture; it is more continuous and persistent than an appeal to the eye.

13. The auditory appeal, more easily than the visual, shapes the congregation into an oriented audience; we have no single name for a group of spectators.

14. Each member of an audience is influenced by his fellows, as well as by the performer; these contributory influences are more likely to come through the sense of sight.

15. General *rapport* is facilitated when the main appeal is to hearing, and the circumstances enable each auditor to see what other auditors are doing.

CHAPTER III

TYPES OF AUDIENCES

THE PROCESS OF ORIENTATION

It is a matter of common experience that the ease with which one yields to the speaker's invitation depends first of all upon the type of audience which the occasion assembles. Although it is true that in some points every audience is unique, it is nevertheless possible to make out certain important features in respect to which audiences may be classified. Thus they might be classified with respect to the age of the individuals composing them, their homogeneity of interest, their education, or their economic status.

The most important of these features is perhaps what Bentley and Woolbert have called the degree and type of "polarization." Thus Woolbert [72] writes:

"To make an audience, there must be 'polarization,' the setting opposite of two objects. This it is that makes of a group an audience. Typically the audience and the speaker face in opposite directions; their minds take different bents: they are moving in opposing channels. Even though they be strongly of 'one mind' on some points, the very nature of the conditions is such as to place them at opposite poles.

"In the psychological study of the audience we have to consider four kinds of relationship: (*1*) that of the whole group to itself,—the 'all-to-all'; (*2*) that of the group to the speaker or performer,—the 'all-to-one'; (*3*) that of the speaker or performer to the group before him,—the 'one-to-all'; and (*4*) that of the speaker to each individual in the audience,—the 'one-to-one' relations."

Bentley,[6] who has given special study to the various forms of human congregation, gives a detailed analysis of the various forms of integration, their conditions and results. Distinguishing between the audience and the mob, he writes as follows:

"In the audience, the meaning of the discourse tends to strengthen the individual relations of the mass to the speaker, who represents the topic; in the polarized mob, the significant conditions tend, on the other hand, to increase the relations within the mass, or the secondary pole, of the group. Strong interrelations among the members of the mass form the first and primary characteristic of the mob; strong individual relations between the speaker and the other members, the first and primary characteristic of the audience."

Classifying such congregates of human beings on the basis of their degree of integration, Bentley indicates the important differences between such levels as are represented in the following progressive stages:

"Casual and unstudied aggregates" (the railway platform at train time being an example).

"Temporary and spontaneous gatherings whither individuals are drawn by a common object of curiosity" (such as a fallen horse or a damaged machine).

"Congregates which are led or governed. There is a spokesman to give expression or a leader to harangue, to initiate, and to command. Such groups are polarized."

"The *selected and primed* audience, the meetings, *e.g.*, of religious, fraternal, and social 'organizations.' "

". . . the Anglo-Saxon form of trial by jury. United for a special end, the jurors are expected to ponder until they 'are of one mind,' despite the mental differences which mark them as men. . . . We must look to organizations of this sort, presenting the greatest unity amid wide inherent diversity, for illustrations of our final grade. . . ."

As instructive as these classifications are, they do not entirely serve our present purpose, which does not extend to all these degrees of social integration. Instead we can to advantage bear chiefly in mind the resemblances between the performer and the advertisement, and classify audiences essentially on the basis of the tasks with which the performer is confronted when he faces them. But we may make good use of the descriptive term "polarization" which these writers have adopted, or of a somewhat similar term, "orientation," which has certain advantages over the term "polarization." By the term "orientation" we shall mean the establishment of a pattern of attention, when the group is considered, or a set and direction of interest, when we consider the individuals comprising the group. We may then with profit consider the following as the chief types of audiences.

I. THE PEDESTRIAN AUDIENCE

The lowest degree of orientation is represented by such a transient audience as the pedestrians on a busy street, before whom the street-corner orator sets up his box. Each individual is intent upon his special destination and business, and there exist no common ties or lines of communication between the members of the audience nor between the members and the speaker. The task of winning the audience in this case is similar to that of the show window. It involves the very first of the five steps,—catching or diverting the attention, and at least the second,—that of holding interest. Whether or not it goes further depends on the purpose of the speaker. If he is determined to influence votes or to dispose of wares, he must effectively perform the whole series of five tasks.

2. THE DISCUSSION GROUP AND PASSIVE AUDIENCE

With the discussion group we find the first signs of preliminary orientation toward a speaker. When people enter an auditorium, their first polarization is toward the room itself. If they could all be placed in the room at the same moment, we might say that the audience was oriented toward the physical environment. The size of the room, its arrangement, the location of the platform, the decorations, the exits, the seating arrangements and possibilities, the lighting fixtures, etc., command first attention. Ordinarily this orientation readily shifts, and is replaced by polarization of the members of the audience to each other. Each individual becomes conscious of himself as an object of regard by his neighbors, and is in turn prompted to scrutinize other individuals with curiosity and interest. The self-consciousness arising out of this rather formal social situation is indicated externally by the formal posture and bearing of each individual. Each chair is occupied by a self-conscious individual, sitting erect, observing the usual proprieties, glancing covertly at more conspicuous individuals, adjusting wearing apparel to its conventional position, and tending to inhibit such acts as will call attention to one's self. Gradually acquaintances are discovered, signs of recognition are given, comments are exchanged with companions, usually concerning the personnel of the audience. When this second phase of orientation ultimately gives way in favor of polarization toward the speaker, there will be equally obvious signs in the audience. Individuals will slouch in their seats, will ignore apparel that is awry, will cough more freely, and will assume a general attitude of restfulness rather than this one of alertness.

Now in the discussion group, where each member may in turn be speaker, the audience is very transient and unstable. Each member does not usually get his turn, unless special arbitrary rules are enforced to secure this result. Some members have a way of getting the audience related to them more easily, definitely, and frequently than do others. The initial task of diverting the attention is not so conspicuous as in the case of the street audience, nor the related case of the show window. The situation is more like that of the advertisements in a magazine, which are all placed together in an advertising section and segregated from the reading matter. Individuals compete with one another in determining the direction of orientation, although a loosely organized attitude favorable to speakers, in the one case, and to advertisements in the other, remains established in general throughout.

A similar type of audience, so far as its orientation is concerned, is represented by the miscellaneous group, assembled for some common but passive purpose, such as that of being entertained by music or drama, listening to a lecture or debate, or witnessing some performance or spectacle. Amateur night at a vaudeville house is a rather extreme case of this type of audience. The courtesy of the common purpose gives the speaker or performer his chance, and guarantees initial attention. The task of winning the audience does not begin with the first of the five tasks we have indicated, but begins at a point well along in the total process. Maintenance of interest is here the first step, and the process continues to a point determined only by the purpose or the success of the performer. The task here resembles that to be found in the sales letter, personally addressed to one.

3. THE SELECTED AUDIENCE

A further degree of polarization, upon which the speaker can build, is present in the selected audience, assembled for some common purpose of a more active sort, but not all sympathetic one with another or with the speaker's point of view or aim. A meeting of labor delegates, the deliberations of a jury, a session of Congress illustrate this type of orientation. The rules of order and the sincerity of the common purpose take care of the first two steps, in the main. Impression, persuasion, and direction, the last three of the five tasks, characterize the speaker's undertaking here. The task is comparable to that of the catalogue description of an article, which seeks to determine only which variety or brand of a commodity will be purchased by the individual who is already influenced to buy one or other of several competing wares.

4. THE CONCERTED AUDIENCE

When the audience assembles with a concerted, active purpose, with sympathetic interest in a mutual enterprise, but with no clear division of labor or rigid organization of authority, the degree of polarization is already almost complete but facile. A college class, intent upon the consideration of an economic, scientific, or literary point, a graduate seminar where mutual inquiry and joint contribution are the object, represent instances. Those not inclined to attend and not interested are either eliminated beforehand or are ignored. The fixing of impressions is taken care of by the device of taking notes, assembling outlines, or utilizing other varieties of memoranda. The main tasks are those of convincing and directing action or thought.

5. THE ORGANIZED AUDIENCE

Complete although perhaps superficial polarization of the audience toward a speaker is illustrated in a team or a company, a military unit or a gymnasium class, organized with a rigid division of labor and authority, supported by specific common purpose and interest, with tasks well learned, and already persuaded to the authority of the leader. A scout leader or a football captain has this perfect polarization of his immediate audience. Nothing remains but the last of the five tasks, the direction of specific action. The relation is like that sustained to a price list, a guide post, or a bill from the dentist.

The characteristics of these five types of audiences may be schematically indicated by the following outline. In each case there is shown, according to the foregoing analysis, the point at which the performer's task commonly begins, and the processes still to be undertaken if the typical tasks are carried to completion.

PEDESTRIAN AUDIENCE	DISCUSSION AND PASSIVE AUDIENCE	SELECTED AUDIENCE	CONCERTED AUDIENCE	ORGANIZED AUDIENCE
Attention	. . . .	. . . .	. . . .	. . . .
Interest	Interest	. . . .	. . . .	. . . .
Impression	Impression	Impression	. . . .	. . . .
Conviction	Conviction	Conviction	Conviction	. . . .
Direction	Direction	Direction	Direction	Direction

6. THE ABSENT AUDIENCE

It may be well to call attention to another use of the word "audience," to indicate a type of situation which does not properly come into our present discussion. The writer is accustomed to refer to his audience, as is also the editor, the publisher, the artist, and perhaps even the architect. In this connection the word "audience" is merely a collective term, used to indicate the absent and isolated individuals who will at some time or usually at different times be the observers of the produced work. There is of course usually no aggregation or congregation of people involved, and hence the group phenomena which an assembled audience may display will be missing. Nevertheless the existence of these "patrons," as they might better be called, exercises its influence on the performer; and to some extent the knowledge on the part of each patron that others will sometime view the product and be influenced individually by it, may have some influence on the reactions of each. But this group of patrons does not constitute an audience in our present sense of that word. It lacks the essential characteristic of a strictly *social* situation, in which the individuals must be influenced not only by a common stimulus but also by one another.

The special characteristic of such a group of patrons is the fact that the appeal is presented to them through but one of the various avenues of perception,—as the visual, the auditory, usually. The modern radio audience is a good illustration of such a group. Only the auditory sense is appealed to by the performance or even by relevant features of the surroundings. Stimuli to the other senses may be distracting and irrelevant. The listener's neighbors may be intent upon other subjects; his fellow listeners are remote in space, as is the performer also. There is therefore little of the orientation process in such a case, and although the performer may find numerous psychological problems in addressing such a scattered group, there is little to be said with respect to the audience as a phenomenon. There is indeed no essential difference between this type of audience and that of the writer, publisher, or artist.

THE ORIENTATION OF THE SPEAKER

The goal of the speaker is thus, abstracting from his specific purpose, the orientation of his audience toward himself. This necessitates his action toward each member of the group, rather than toward the group as a unit. The group, and therefore the audience, is an unreal abstraction. People in general are not general people. There is no oversoul possessed by the audience, to which the speaker may appeal; but, instead, there are particular individuals, each psychologically related to the speaker and to surrounding individuals. To be sure, the members of the audience influence one another. One member, failing in attention or interest, distracts his neighbors by his wrongly oriented behavior. The intent interest of a neighbor also restrains the flighty attention of the disturber. But if the speaker merely addresses the crowd as a whole, failing to take into account the individuals of which it is comprised, his speech can scarcely avoid the automatic and inflexible character of a reproduction. He tends to become a fixture in the landscape, competing with other inert objects for the polarization of the group. Only a frankly recitative performance or the timid speaker who appears under protest and wishes merely to survive the ordeal can afford to become such a fixture.

The speaker's orientation toward the individual members of the audience is even more necessary in our own time than it was in earlier days, when traditions inclined toward exaggerated eloquence, attitudinizing, and bombast to a degree which would not now be tolerated. Only obliviousness to the individual persons before one could enable the average speaker to indulge in these abandoned flights. Consciousness of individual auditors, while it may restrain fancy, encourages earnestness, directness, and simplicity.

THE AUDIENCE AS A *GESTALT*

A mystical movement in modern psychology, known as "gestalt-theorie" would take exception to the foregoing analysis. In fact this school of psychology eschews all analysis, or would like to do so. For them, discussion of the audience and performer would require first that a position be taken so far away from the facts that the details could not be clearly observed. The audience would appear as one vast blur, with which the performer would be merged. Discussion would then necessarily relate only to this vague whole or total blur. We may in fact quote an account of the psychology of the audience as given from this point of view by Wheeler.[70]

"The individual and the group constitute an organic unit. . . . Consider a lecturer speaking before an audience. He does not pause to scrutinize each individual face or to analyze the movements of each person; he does not hear the scuffling of individual feet. On the contrary he grasps the total situation at once, apprehending the attitude of the group as a whole toward him. . . . In any event the stimulus to which the speaker is reacting is the group, and not its individual members. It is an ensemble of noises, gesture and movements, not any isolated occurrence."

This conception of the audience as a blur is even carried to the point of designating the group, not figuratively, as we all do, but descriptively, as "it." Thus:

"Had it not been inhibited by fear of breaking a long-established custom and thus subjecting itself to criticism, the audience would have walked out to relieve itself of this strain, but courtesy prompted it to remain in the hall and to make the best of it."

The strain (the feeling of indifference) and the walking are thus not attributed to the individual auditors but to the audience "as a whole." Since, however, the speaker and the audience have been said to be "an organic unit," we should expect the speaker also to be indifferent and to walk out with the audience; an organic unit should surely act in a unitary way.

The fact is that ideas of this kind rest merely on the question whether description is to be from a remote point of view (as the sociologist would undertake it) or from as close a station as the psychologist may adopt. Thus from a distant point of view we could describe the audience as awake or asleep. Suppose we say the audience is asleep. Coming closer we might observe individuals; most of them would be asleep as individuals, but here and there would be a wakeful one. Is the audience then asleep or not? Clearly, if we get close enough to the facts, the audience is not an organic unit, but an assemblage.

On the other hand, much the same thing may be said of the individual. Observing him as an "organic whole" we may say, "He is asleep." Yet even the soundest sleeper is not *entirely* asleep. Some of his systems are in abeyance; others, such as heart and lungs, are active enough; he may even be "talking in his sleep" or dreaming; he may respond promptly to some signals but not to others. Is he then asleep or not? Clearly enough, if we get close to the individual, we find that he is not an organic unit in the absolute sense, but an assemblage of loosely organized systems. Physiology would be able to show that even these "systems" are not clean-cut organic wholes.

The fact is that it is just these differences in remoteness of viewpoint that distinguish the various sciences, such as sociology, psychology, physiology, and chemistry. What is the lowest level of analysis for one science may appear as a mysticism to another science. Psychology is characterized by a point of view sufficiently near at hand to enable it to get a clear picture of the individual.

The line is not hard and fast, and it is not easy to draw; the position in fact varies with the interests and temperament of different psychologists, and with the nature of the problem. Discerning the individual clearly, psychology is nevertheless interested in his relations with other individuals, also clearly discerned. It is also interested in a partial analysis of the individual into component activities and functions.

For our own purpose the point of view that takes the performer-and-audience as an "organic whole" and as the final unit of analysis remains mysticism. Nothing can be done about such a picture but to engage in ecstatic exclamations concerning the wonders of such "totals." We shall instead be interested in individuals and their relations one to another, and in at least the first step of analysis which makes it possible to consider the individual as in himself not wholly an "all or none" system.

For our purpose, if there are "feelings of indifference," they will be in individual observers. If any "walking out" is done, it will not be on the part of the "audience as a whole" but by those whose legs engage in the activity. The "members" of the audience are thus to be considered, in their orientation to one another and to the performer, who in turn is oriented toward the individuals comprising the audience.

Only in one whose usual experience is that of stage-fright, or who removes himself from human affairs to so great a distance that he no longer discerns people but only "men as trees walking" can the "gestalt" account make any contribution at all to the psychology of the audience.

PRACTICAL CONCLUSIONS

1. Every audience is unique, yet it is possible to indicate a limited number of typical audiences, and it is important that the performer classify his audience correctly.

2. The type of an audience depends most of all upon the nature of its orientation toward the performer,—upon the phenomena of polarization.

3. Orientation depends chiefly upon the point in the series of five steps at which the performance begins and the step at which it ends.

4. With the "pedestrian audience" the very first step, catching attention, is primary; how much further the process goes varies with the purpose of the performer.

5. With the "passive audience" or "discussion group" the first task is usually already accomplished, or guaranteed by rules of order; the performer's initial problem is more likely to be the second step,—holding attention or interest; how far the process goes again depends upon the occasion or the success of the performer.

6. With the "selected audience" the primary task may well be the third one,—impressiveness; this may or may not give way to the fourth and fifth steps.

7. With the "concerted audience" the performer typically begins with the first three steps already accomplished; conviction, and perhaps direction, are his chief responsibilities.

8. With the "organized audience" the performer has only to issue instructions; attention, interest, impression, and conviction may usually be taken for granted.

9. The primary virtue of the performer is to understand clearly which of these tasks will be confronted at the start, and how far through the succeeding stages it is his duty to carry the audience.

10. The tasks involved, as well as the initial and terminal

points, are determined by the nature of the occasion, the purpose of the performer, and the preliminary preparation of the audience.

11. The first goal of the performer is to make sure that the audience is oriented effectively toward himself or his materials.

12. The audience can be treated as a unit only in impersonal performances (gymnastics, music) or in cases of exaggerated oratory and grandiloquence.

13. Explicit observation of individual members of the audience, though it may restrain fancy and inhibit rhetoric, does nevertheless promote earnestness, directness, and simplicity.

14. The audience as a whole is a mere verbal abstraction; actually there are only the separate individuals with their personal behaviors and mutual influences.

CHAPTER IV

A Typical Situation

With these various facts in mind, can analysis yield any useful points or suggestions? Is there anything in the way of scientific observations that has a bearing on the process of polarization that is not already the well-worn property of common sense and practice?

Perhaps the most useful and immediate suggestion is the warning to go before the audience with as full knowledge as possible of the mode and degree of its polarization. The performer should know clearly beforehand just the point in the five tasks where his work is to begin, and the extent to which the complete series of tasks is to be sustained or carried by the performance. A further suggestion would be for the performer to be prepared to shift his notion of the audience and to vary his mode of attack if he should find that his preconceived idea was in error. As obvious as these suggestions are, their violation is quite sure to be the downfall of many attempts of the young speaker or performer, or of the specialized speaker in an unfamiliar setting.

The situation can best be made clear by a concrete example in which various degrees of success or failure were seen to depend on the degree of recognition of and preparedness for such circumstances. Almost any series of speakers before a given audience will afford illustrations. The following instance is one of many that have been carefully observed.

DEGREES OF SUCCESS AND FAILURE

A young college teacher was once called on to address an organization of prominent publishers and business men. On the program with him were a famous political orator and a woman of conspicuous local publicity in social and political affairs. The topic assigned the professor was "Advertising and Progress." He anticipated a fairly homogeneous group of intelligent men, assembled in the form of an ordinary informal lecture audience, and oriented beforehand toward the appearance of the speaker and the topic of discussion. He prepared a careful and sober historical and interpretative account of the field indicated by his topic, calculated to explain and instruct, and to make a more or less permanent impression and contribution to the topic, for an audience looking for information.

Arriving at the scene of the session, he was dismayed to find an enormous banquet hall, with miscellaneous invited guests in the balconies, tables spread with food, drink, and souvenirs, many of the latter of a noisy variety. Small table groups were packed into the room, each engaged in its special form of frivolity. Half of the audience was thus seated with backs to the speakers' table. Local vaudeville artists on a side stage contributed their share to the festivities.

In the midst of this excitement the chairman arose and, with much effort to make himself heard above the din of dishes, bottles, and voices, announced that the professor had come from a distant city to address them on "Advertising and Progress." In the tentative lull that came at this moment, the professor arose as the first speaker of the evening. He was a short man, not much more than twice the height of the table behind which he stood. He began his serious résumé of the march of history as related to the function of publicity. As the din increased, he raised his voice so that he could always at least hear his own words. The set logical theme forbade impromptu resources, even if they had been in the speaker's repertoire.

The speaker had come in the mode of a classified advertisement, to impress, persuade, and direct. Instead, he was called upon, by the situation that faced him, to divert and interest, in the mode of a show window. He had expected an audience of the third or fourth type. Instead, he faced a seated but mentally pedestrian audience of the first type. Lacking the physical advantages, the native eloquence, the established platform prestige, the contemporary public interest, and the ready versatility of his fellow speakers, he struggled on until he could no longer endure the futility of his performance. He ceased speaking and sat down, without having, in any perceptible way, affected the conduct of the banqueters.

THE UNDERLYING FACTORS

His efforts had, as a matter of fact, oriented toward the speakers' table a few members of the audience, who chanced to sit facing it. The second speaker, who now arose, was also favored by the reluctant accession of courtesy accorded a woman orator by a group of reveling males. With a ready adaptability she abandoned entirely the topic for which she had been announced, and for which she had prepared. She set out at once upon an anecdotal account of her inside knowledge of certain local events of public importance, and concluded with a few generalizations on the subject she had originally intended to discuss.

The first speaker had completely failed to win the

audience. This second speaker succeeded in polarizing the audience toward her own person. If time had permitted and her energy sufficed, she could have led her auditors on to the theme of her original purpose. As compared with the first performer, her success was definite, and it was due to her readier perception of the nature of the audience and her greater versatility in shifting her performance in terms of this perception.

The third speaker was the internationally famous political orator. He found the audience, by the time he arose, quietly digesting its food, with chairs turned toward the speakers' table. Supported by his dominating voice, his eloquence, and by the natural physique and the prestige which were his, he began at that point in the series of tasks at which the second speaker had retired, and which the first speaker had never reached.

The first speaker had been unable to displace the attention of the audience from its internal polarization. Each member was oriented toward nearby objects and adjacent members. The second speaker was able to catch attention, to hold interest, and at least to fix the impression of her own presence, when her time expired. The third performer was able to take these first three steps for granted, and to set out at once upon the tasks of convincing and directing action.

The episode not only illustrates the general analysis we have made, but shows up in clear relief the reality and inexorableness of the five points or tasks in the winning of an audience.

SUCCESS WITHOUT INSIGHT

A public performance may succeed only because of the sheer intrinsic interest of its materials; but even then its effectiveness may be promoted by conformity to the psychology of the situation. With given materials the difference between success and failure may be due to psychological factors alone. Even with the best of intentions on the part of performer and audience, violation of important principles may prevent the teamwork both may be eager to develop.

It does not follow that a formal acquaintance with these principles will guarantee their effective application. And public performers who have never paused to make such an analysis may nevertheless be among the most successful. In such cases we should expect to find one or more of three conditions:

1. The subject matter itself had such strong interest that it over-weighed the importance of principles.

2. The performer was fortunately gifted with natural talents, with impressive features, with high prestige, or with strong personal charm.

3. The performer unwittingly, through an uncommon sense of fitness or through the use of methods sanctioned on the basis of tradition or experience, actually conformed to psychological principles without formulating them.

A boy in his 'teens was an active member of the church in his country town, and taught a rural school in an adjoining section. The local minister, being called away for a few days, asked the youngster to lead the mid-week prayer meeting of the adults. The boy replied that he would not know what to do or say, before all those old folks. The preacher's reassuring promise was, "The Lord will put words into your mouth."

In the face of this guarantee there was nothing for a believer to do but to undertake the leadership. But doubts soon arose, and as he walked back and forth from town to the country schoolhouse, the boy began to lay plans which might save him from embarassment in case the promised words should fail to make their miraculous appearance.

An opening talk was planned in which life was likened to this daily traveled road; analogies were found between bits of geography along the route and the burdens and temptations of the parishioners; craftily the scripture lesson, the hymns, and their sequence were mapped out in advance; the probable audience was considered, and prayers and testimonials scheduled in terms of the personal characteristics, idiosyncrasies, and influences of the individuals.

When the critical evening arrived, the boy, finding no other message "put into his mouth," fell back perforce on his own humble program. There was an outpouring of fervor among the devotees that overwhelmed the congregation, prolonged the services to an unwonted hour, and awakened a revival spirit that carried into later sessions.

The elders were warm in their approval; they spoke of prophecy fulfilled, for "A little child shall lead them." They were sure that a more than human power had rallied to their service in the preacher's lamented absence. The youthful chairman, however, knowing the mortal source and the deliberate design of the program, found his thoughts turned in less orthodox directions.

He was struck by the predictable character of human feelings, and the possibility of engineering them; his plans for a clerical career were interrupted in favor of a wholly secular interest in the human mind, including the psychology of the audience. It appeared to him that if untutored but designing manipulation of stimuli, such as verses, hymns, and prayers, could so mislead the elders of his church, principles must be involved that might yield to scientific analysis and statement.

In such a case no explicit consciousness of the performer's tasks was achieved. A rough insight into the total situation and a close acquaintance with the selected and sympathetic members of the audience served the purpose well enough. In most cases such support cannot be counted on; more depends on the performer's own resources; awareness of the typical steps and of any general laws relating to them may be more valuable.

PRACTICAL CONCLUSIONS

1. Before appearing before the audience, the performer ought to secure as full knowledge as possible of the mode and degree of its polarization or orientation at the beginning of the session.

2. The performer should then formulate tentatively his conception of the point in the five steps at which the performance should begin and the distance through them to which the performance is to be carried.

3. The performer must be prepared to shift tactics if the first reactions of the audience show that this tentative preliminary judgment was wrong; the performer must assume the adaptability, rather than expect the audience to accommodate its attitude promptly to his prearranged plan.

4. If the audience fails to move ahead through the successive steps with the performer, the fault lies with the performer.

5. Do not let performance habits and habits of preparation become so crystallized by one type of situation that tactics cannot be shifted with facility when the emergency requires.

6. Do not expect to take the whole audience with you at once; there will usually be refractory members, but if a nucleus can be started the rest may easily fall into line if the performance does not move too fast for them.

7. Formal acquaintance with principles does not guarantee their effective application; practice them repeatedly and consciously until you need not think of them by name, until they appear to become "second nature" to you.

8. Do not trust to "common sense" unless you happen to be that rare creature, a born leader. Common sense is most often nonsense.

9. Paramount in importance is the intrinsic interest of the performance; if this is strong, the details of strategy can more safely be ignored; but the performer should not confuse his personal interest with the interest of the audience.

10. It is the interests of the audience that are most important; but if the performer is keenly interested, this interest is likely to be infectious if it can only be made apparent.

CHAPTER V

SECURING AN AUDIENCE

We may now consider these five tasks in turn, asking what definite suggestions may be offered that may be of assistance in their effective fulfillment. We begin with the first task,—that of catching attention.

MECHANICAL AND INTEREST DEVICES

The teacher, on entering the room where the class is already assembled, busy in conversation or looking out of the window, must polarize the group of individuals into an audience. Attention is to be diverted from its present varied directions and focused upon the teacher and the enterprise now to be begun. In the absence of rigid discipline, compelling personality, fear, or pre-organization by an assistant, various methods may be observed in use.

One speaker advances to the appropriate spot and begins to talk. This effects no reaction. The voice may be raised until its intensity exceeds that of other stimuli, and breaks in upon the attention of the prospective auditors. But then, unless the early remarks made by the teacher have been meaningless, they must be repeated. This method of winning the attention has little to commend it.

Another teacher, saving his breath at least, jangles the desk bell noisily, pounds on the desk with the ruler, or in some similar way competes with other auditory stimuli. Such purely mechanical devices are awkward, irrelevant, and undignified. They predispose the audience to distraction by similar stimuli from the outside and at the most appeal only to shallow reflex curiosity or rely on the authority to which they direct attention.

A very simple rule will assist in such a situation. If, for example, a sound is to be used as an initial attention device, to compete with other distracting sounds, the appeal should then be as far removed from the sheer mechanical level as is possible. This may be done, for example, by using as an attention device, not a louder sound, but one of different quality, or a striking rhythm, or a serial pattern. Thus chimes, mild siren effects, ascending or descending scales, bugles, bells, and the like may be rendered effective even on a relatively low level of intensity. The mechanical level of competition for attention is best illustrated by the matching of one voice against others, one bell or horn against other bells or horns, and so on.

But a third teacher may be observed not to rely on such mechanical devices at all. He takes his place on the platform. Merely taking this position is of course ineffective unless attention is already directed toward it. But add to this some silent but unconventional act, such as simply raising the hand, and polarization is likely to set in smoothly enough. Two or three of the individuals catch this sign and attend to it, ceasing their clamor. This cessation itself attracts the attention of neighbors, who imitatively look in the suggested direction and similarly adopt an attentive attitude. Such polarization, even if it should be a bit slower than that evoked by mechanical pounding, is nevertheless more genuine, relevant, and profound. It does not degrade the personality of the teacher by putting him in a class with mechanical noises, nor does it put him to the humiliation of being required to repeat his preliminary remarks. And it suggests for the remainder of the period an atmosphere of peace rather than one of storm. We may call this method the use of an interest incentive, rather than a mechanical device.

VISUAL VERSUS AUDITORY INTRODUCTIONS

It is on this principle of the interest incentive that the transient or pedestrian audience is most effectively won for initial attention. Some striking act or gesture, the choice of a strategic position, a peculiarity of garb, a curious object held in the hand, in general some visual appeal to curiosity or other native interest best focuses upon the speaker the attention of the pedestrian audience. Initial attention or polarization to the speaker is almost always visual in its mode, and with the transition, from visual attention to the speaker's appearance or act, to auditory attention to his remarks, goes the shift from the first task, that of catching attention, to the second, that of holding it, or arousing interest.

It seems in general to be a valid principle that initial attention to the speaker should be directed visually, rather than in terms of sound, especially if the distracting stimuli are auditory in character. Something about the shift from one sensory field to the other seems to facilitate a general mental shift in the direction of orientation. On similar principles attention can best be called to a new act in a spectacle or circus by a preliminary warning to the ear, for here the competing distractions are visual in their appeal, and it is clear that visual attention to one direction is a bar to visual stimuli appearing at other places.

This simple principle of attracting attention through a different sense than that through which it is to be held seems actually to have evolved as an empirical rule in many situations. The blast of a trumpet presages the appearance of the procession; the gong or bell announces the beginning of the tableau; the bugler foretells the lowering of the flag. On the other hand, the dimming of a light, or the raising of a curtain prepares for the beginning of the spoken drama; a more or less formal and impressive entrance introduces the opera; the speaker declares, by advancing to the front of the platform or by raising his hand, his intention presently to speak.

The psychological factors underlying this principle seem to be the following. In the case of the speaker, for example (or any auditory attraction), the attempt to compete with other auditory stimuli involves too great a displacement of the attention of the audience. But since the eyes of the auditors are either unoccupied or at least are mobile and constantly shifting, it is relatively easy to capture visual attention. This very shift constitutes a half-way accomplishment of the speaker's desire. Competing auditory stimuli now being weakened by the relatively easier visual appeal, the remaining shift back to a new auditory appeal is thus a transition step, which divides the difficult task of securing attention into two easier stages. In the same way, in the circus the shift of visual regard is effected in the round about way. The blast of the trumpet, an auditory appeal to relatively unoccupied sense organs, constitutes the transition event, which divides the process into two easier steps.

There are thus actually two principles or suggestions involved here. On the one hand the rule seems to be to appeal through a different sense than that to which attention is to be subsequently confined. On the other hand there is the general rule that it is easier to attract attention through an unoccupied sensory channel than through one at the moment actively engaged. There is some reason for supposing that the second rule is the more genuine, the former being only a description of what happens in cases in which the sense to be ultimately held is the one that is at the moment actively engaged elsewhere. If for example the audience is at the moment engrossed in observing visually some spectacle, and the ultimate aim is to hold the attention to an auditory appeal, there seems to be no reason why the initial appeal should not be direct to the unoccupied sense of hearing.

A further point of importance is that mechanical devices are relatively more effective with younger, stupider, and less well-informed audiences than they are with the older, more intelligent, and better educated. The younger and duller are less able to appreciate the subtleties of verbal meanings and the mild flow of facial expression and symbolic gesture of the restrained type. They are both more interested in and more effectively impressed by concrete presentations which either duplicate or imitatively portray the actual situations under discussion. It is for this reason, as we shall see at a later point, that various visual aids, in the way of motion pictures and the like, have their effectiveness increased when they are substituted, in the case of the immature and the relatively dull, for verbal descriptions.

CHANNELS OF DISPERSION AND COMMUNICATION

Classroom teachers have often, at the beginning of a new school term, to consider the problem of seat assignments, a problem which involves in a complex way many of the principles of audience formation. Shall last year's location be retained by each pupil, or shall a new seating arrangement be adopted? The problem has conflicting aspects.

On the one hand, new assignments mean excitement, loss of time, and for some pupils, a period of distraction until adaptation sets in to the new environment. On the other hand, by the end of the preceding term a complex set of channels of communication and directions of interest had become established. These channels of dispersion facilitate concerted action, and render easy and swift the propagation of mischief as well as the spread of attention.

Some pupils or some locations are centers of influence, and the question is whether the best results will accrue from preserving these centers or compelling new ones to become established. The pedagogical problem is considered here only by way of showing what is meant by channels of communication. But in a more general form we may inquire what are the usual channels of dispersion throughout an audience.

How does the speaker's influence spread from the platform and through the audience? Does it move backward, wave-like, from the front central position, curving out to the edges and back to the rear of the crowd? Or does it move with fits and starts, and from such transient centers of influence as may have been established during the preliminary orientation of the auditors to one another?

Such features will no doubt vary with the audience and with the nature of the influence, and little careful observation of the matter has been reported. Preliminary experiments on a college class have been reported by Clark.[12] The students watched the instructor preparing liquids (actually water only) from which, it was intimated, a new odor might emerge. "Each individual was asked to record his seat number and the time elapsing before he smelled the new odor." One fifth of the 168 students gave positive reports, and since there was no

question of the actual distribution of an odor, the sequence and location of positive reports are used as an
indication of the spread of the suggested effect.

The reaction times increased as the rows become more
remote from the speaker's station, but this cannot be
said to be relevant to the situation of the typical audience, because of the peculiar nature of the supposed communication (an odor). The chief (and tentative) conclusions suggested by the experimenter are:

1. That the members of a group are more readily "influenced by verbal instructions" than is the isolated auditor.

2. That "instead of proceeding by regular waves, the influence of the leader first affects a number of especially susceptible
persons in the order of the favorableness of their positions . . .
then radiates from them for a certain period of time."

3. "That there are clearly marked spatial and temporal
optima for the influences exerted upon the crowd. In this experiment such optima were the second half minute and approximately the eighth seat from the right in the third row."

This single experiment of course yields no results for
audiences in general. It may be that each audience must
be described in terms of its own more or less accidentally
placed centers of influence,—auditors with marked susceptibility or high prestige. The study of the spread
of other types of influence, such as the attention to intro-
ductory words, applause, laughing, coughing, excitement,
and the like, should yield interesting data bearing on the
general problems raised by Clark's experiment. Such
principles might well be given deliberate attention by
those interested in successful audience formations. Indeed, the box-office need not be an isolated institution,
but may be skillfully annexed by the platform as one
of the effective instruments of the repertoire.

Experimental studies suggest that even so simple a factor as the location of an individual in the audience definitely affects the task of attention getting, or perhaps of attention holding.   These experiments are thus summarized by Griffith:[25]

"In a study of the grades gotten by university students who were seated in different parts of a room, it was found that students on the outskirts of an audience were more apt to get a low grade than students in the center.   Since lower averages fell not only at the back but at the sides and even at the very front of an audience, the inability to hear the lecturer or see the demonstration could not be invoked.   Moreover the center area of high averages traveled with the size of the audience so that in a large audience the area of high grades very often coincided with the area of low grades for a small audience.

"From these and from other facts the conclusion was drawn that individual differences in performance may be due to the degree of social integration.   Individuals in the periphery of a crowd are apt to be restless and inattentive to whatever may be attracting the interest of the main group, whereas physical compactness and the interests and activities of a group polarized toward the speaker may knit together the main body of an audience.   In other words, the heart of an audience is organized not only toward the speaker but with respect to itself.   Its internal organization favors individual achievement."

PRACTICAL CONCLUSIONS

1. Mechanical devices for catching initial attention are not only undignified; they also predispose the audience to distraction by similar mechanical but irrelevant stimuli.

2. Catch initial attention by an appeal to a different quality from that operating at the moment, rather than by one differing only in intensity.

3. Intrinsically interesting incentives are more effective than mechanical signals to attention, for they lead spontaneously toward the second step,—the maintenance of interest.

4. Initial attention is most effectively attracted by appeal through a sensory channel other than that in terms of which the performance is to be continued.

5. Sounds most effectively introduce the visual spectacle, and visual signals best call attention to the spoken performance.

6. It is easier to attract attention through a sensory channel not at the moment occupied in the activity of the audience.

7. The younger, duller, and more poorly informed the audience, the greater will be the value of mechanical appeals or signals for initial attention.

8. The influence of the performer does not travel across the audience in concentric circles, nor in waves, nor in straight lines of advance; it proceeds zig-zag to the most susceptible centers or persons, from which points it radiates in local areas.

9. Do not be misled by the behavior of random members of the audience; try first to locate the susceptible centers of influence and in the beginning be guided by them.

10. In an audience seated at random, the most susceptible points are likely to be those near the center of the group; but in many audiences those seeking seats well to the front are likely to be the most ready to react and the most favorably disposed.

11. Inattentiveness in the center of the audience is a bad sign; restlessness or inattention on the edges of the crowd are more natural and should give less concern in the beginning.

CHAPTER VI

HOLDING THE AUDIENCE

MAINTAINING INTEREST

Attention once caught must be maintained, and this is the second step in winning the audience. We must, for our purpose, abstract from the subject matter which the speaker or other performer presents. The only elementary principles bearing on subject matter would become meaningless because of their generality and obviousness. Aside from having something interesting to say or do, which is after all the fundamental consideration, there are certain methods of presentation that are more effective than others. We are interested at this point not in impressing, persuading, or directing the audience, but merely in maintaining attention to the performer.

General advice offered to intending public performers is most likely to be in connection with this task,—that of maintaining interest. Such advice is likely to cover points which only fortunate hereditary endowment could provide. The following general rules are suggested by Overstreet,[53] a practiced and effective public speaker:

1. Do not be an unloader. . . .
2. Think of your audience.
3. Look *at* your audience. . . .
4. Find what interests *them*.
5. Think along with your audience. . . . . . .
6. Use humor humorously.
7. Keep off the monotone. . . .
8. Eliminate distressing mannerisms.
9. Do not be a flat-land mind. .
10. Nor a string-of-beads mind.
11. Never make an audience feel inferior. . . . . . .
12. Keep your audience thinking along with you.

51

13. Never be angry at the audi-
    ence, only with them. . .
14. Cultivate a voice that can be
    endured.
15. Do not let your appearance
    occupy the foreground. . .
16. Avoid the commonplace and the
    bizarre.
17. Organize your speech into
    groups and larger groups. .
18. Give an effect of rhythmic move-
    ment.
19. Let your speech march . .
20. Close with a snap!

MUSCULAR METHODS

Many speakers rely on purely muscular devices or at least make much use of them or fail to avoid them. One is full of gesticulation and movement, paces the floor, swings his body, threshes about with his arms, exaggerates the variations in pitch and intensity of voice. He may even perform antics, such as standing on one leg, kicking, switching his coat-tails, waving his handkerchief, pounding the desk, or leaping upon the table.

Another, without this mechanical exaggeration, and with a more restrained muscular repertoire, and with a natural range of intonation, succeeds in conveying that vague and interesting impression which the audience describes as "personality."

The general rule is clear, and again it is consonant with experimental results from the study of printed appeals. The mechanical devices are relatively poor, since they are after all irrelevant, and attract attention not to the theme but to its distracting background. They are to be used, as in advertising, only when interest incentives are wanting. Experiments show that "poor copy" is much improved in attention value and in degree and duration of interest by such mechanical devices as position, contrast, intensity, and white space. But these devices make little or no contribution to the value of appeals that are intrinsically interesting.

The poor personality, in the same way, may profit by posture, gesture, position, and antic, and by forced variations in intonation. But in general these should be avoided, and the personality that can succeed only by virtue of them should seek vocational direction.

EFFECTIVE *RAPPORT*

Undoubtedly the first step after the initial introduction is for the speaker to make sure of the existence of *rapport* between himself and his auditors. If he is sure of their confidence in him, and of their probable sustained interest in the subject matter of what he has to say, he can begin at once, without any time-wasting preliminaries. If the audience really came for the purpose of hearing him, rather than for that of banqueting; if his reputation as an expert on his topic is familiar to the audience; if his coming has been well heralded, so as to arouse an attitude of expectancy and sympathy; if the circumstances or occasion of his appearance are of a serious nature; if in appearance and manner he does not positively repel the sympathies of his hearers;—in such cases he may well dispense with all seductive measures and get down to business.

But if the audience is known to be suspicious or antagonistic or blasé; if his introduction has not been well engineered; if his own confidence is weak; or if the circumstances of his appearance do not suggest serious and sustained consideration;—then he may well act otherwise. In such cases it is well to tide over the shifting period of polarization from visual appearance to oral discourse by promoting a general atmosphere of *rapport*. An amusing story that is relevant, an apt reaction to the chairman's introduction, reference to a topic of current interest, or to a universal motive or idea have just this virtue. They arouse emotions favorable for group solidarity, sentiments that are approved and identified with the speaker, a *rapport* that includes both narrator and listener. Meanwhile they carry over the initial attention from the visual to the auditory field. The use of such techniques is too common to call for further comment.

It is sometimes pointed out that the usual audience suffers from an inferiority feeling, due to the subordination of movements, the sole appropriation of the opportunity for expression, by the performer, by his elevation on a platform, and other like considerations. And it has been urged that the performer's first step in securing *rapport* should be the dispelling of this feeling of subordination.

Some speakers commonly do this. Thus they begin with a few remarks deprecating their own right to instruct the audience; they offer flattering remarks or narrate complimentary incidents dealing with the personnel of the audience, their appearance, their loyalty, the architecture of their homes, the cleanliness of their city. Or instead they relate some episode which at once puts the speaker in an amusing light or suggests that after all he is only human.

It is true that usually the audience assembles to hear something they do not already know, or to witness something the like of which they cannot themselves accomplish. The mechanical arrangements of the usual auditorium also further the relative humility which these facts are likely to imply. But it is far from true that this feeling should at once be dispelled.

The technique of ceremonial and regalia which is so much employed in courts, in churches, lodges, and schoolrooms is deliberately calculated to enhance the prestige of the performer or leader. If the occasion is one for impression or conviction, it is often true that the feeling of inferiority on the part of the audience should be fostered and capitalized. Only in occasional instances of persuasion, and in cases where entertainment or mild instruction is the aim, does it seem desirable to dispel such feeling of subordination as may characterize the audience at the time of its assembly.

Popular accounts of the behavior of audiences such as those of the theater and church often attribute *rapport* to mystical or supernatural influences. Thus a recent writer [5] refers to "the mysterious co-relation of mind and spirit which exists between actor and audience," and to "the *élan vital* which the forces out front send rushing across the footlights to the actor." It is even asserted that "there is only one explanation of the mental intercommunication between actor and audience, and that is the existence of actual psychic waves through the intervening air."

If one were writing only for scientifically informed readers, it would be unnecessary to consider such idle talk. But what writer knows who is likely to read his book and to require his correction? The communication between performer and audience is of course limited to visual and auditory observation. The radio performance is no exception to this rule. It is limitation of attention to visual and auditory clues that guides *rapport*. Even those emotional states of approval, interest, sympathy, amusement, apathy, and protest that help to constitute the particular *rapport* attitude are indicated only by visual and auditory signs. It is sound waves and light waves that "pass over the footlights," not *élan vital*. But these are actually signs; that is, they contribute, to the responsive, information of the complex conditions which, as we say, "they express." And again, as signs, they may arouse appropriate emotions in the listener or in the beholder.

It is just for this reason that very slight distractions in the fields of sight and sound may serve to destroy an effect toward which the performer has carefully worked. A foreign sound, a gesture, a motion on the platform or elsewhere in the auditorium or from the outside, may suffice to dispel just that attentive and emotional reaction required for the success of a particular word, act, jest, or comment. Entrance and exit may be equally easily spoiled. And an incidental sound, gesture, or movement, wrongly placed or timed, may prevent a climax which the performer is urgently engineering. Benchley, in the article just referred to, reports his loss to understand his inability to "put over" a particular point in his performance, until after several weeks he observed by chance that a stage-pulley always made a very slight noise at that particular moment. Advancing the particular ineffective line only half a minute made it successful.

To look for explanation of success or failure of *rapport* in "psychic waves" may often lead to a fruitful zeal (in the effort to generate the waves!) which thus appears to justify the hypothesis. But false theories which by chance occasionally lead to gratifying consequences cannot be accepted by the scientific inquirer.

THE LIMITATIONS OF ATTENTION

Relevant to the task of maintaining interest, on its more mechanical side, is the distinct limitation of human attention from the point of view of number. The presence of more than a half dozen interesting persons or objects on the platform invariably conflicts with the speaker's own effort. A small number of such objects favors the speaker, since such shifts of attention as unavoidably come may nevertheless be accommodated in the general direction of the platform, and do not entail attention to foreign parts of the room, nor to other members of the audience.

The speaker's own language may also well recognize the limits of attention span and duration on the part of his auditors. The number of ideas and the number of words in the average sentence employed soon comes to be a fixed characteristic of the speaker. Sentences with an excess of words or ideas mean effort and undue strain on the part of the auditors who comprehend them. They encourage mind-wandering on the one hand or induce fatigue on the other. The speaker, as well as the writer, should in general incline toward short rather than toward long sentences. It is a useful thing for any public speaker to make an actual count of the number of ideas and words in a few hundred consecutive sentences of his discourse. Thus he may know what his own idiosyncrasy is in this respect.

Quantitative studies in comparative literature have shown the fairly recent tendencies to "decrease of predication and of sentence weight" in English prose, and other students have made comments based on these tendencies. "Before the Elizabethan age the number of words to a sentence averaged approximately fifty. Today our authors limit their sentences to an average of about twenty-five," writes one of these.

Scott [60] calls special attention to this point in the following words:

"Sentences are supposed to be the expression of a complete thought. As such there has been a growing reduction of the length of sentences to conform their lengths to the actual units of thought. It may be that there are those who feel our modern sentences to be staccato and disagreeable as they are recited, but most of us appreciate the modern sentence rhythm and dislike the more involved and heavy rhythm of former writers and speakers. A man who desires the best form of sentence for modern audiences should avoid sentences which to many ears seem clumsy, and should also eschew the opposite extreme, else on the one hand he will exhaust and on the other he will disgust."

On one occasion the writer attended, with eager anticipation, a series of lectures on a topic of special interest, given by a distinguished authority in that field. But instead of being engrossed by the discourse, the auditor found it quite impossible to keep his attention on the speaker's remarks. In spite of a keen professional interest in the topic, his attention kept straying to random and irrelevant events and ideas.

In time this very inattention provoked curiosity. A chance observation of a particular sentence in the lecture suggested a special difficulty of apprehension and understanding, arising from its excessive length. Thereupon the auditor counted the words in a series of successive sentences. Nearly every sentence was over fifty words in length, while some contained as many as seventy words. The series of lectures quite failed to hold the attention of the audience, in spite of the prestige of the speaker and the intrinsic appeal of the subject matter. And the reason, as it now clearly appeared, was entirely the reprehensible sentence length adopted by the lecturer.

DIVERSITY AS AN AID TO SUSTAINED ATTENTION

Although there are definite limitations of *scope* in what we call attention and though we can attend maximally to but one object at a time, a certain diversity within this object is favorable. Try to attend to ever so small an object, say one letter of a printed word, continuously for a period of time. It will be found that even within so narrow a scope, attention is *held* to the object only by discovering diversity within it. Attention shifts within the letter, now to this line or curve, now to that. The diversity of items within the letter is what enables attention to limit itself maximally to the letter as a whole. The same thing may be said of any presented object, topic, or performance. Attention is like a bird. Unless there are several branches to its perch, from which it can flit to and fro while yet remaining on that perch, it is likely instead to flit to some foreign object. Well organized diversity is therefore one of the conditions of sustained attention.

It is more difficult to attend steadily to the recital by a single voice, as in a lecture or monologue, than to a dialogue in which the diversity of items is greater. In the staged drama it is still easier to hold the attention of the audience toward the platform; in addition to conversation and action, the actor supplies diversity through gesture and facial expression. In the opera, added details, such as the music, the costume, the singing, the scenery, conspire with the dialogue, the action, and the movement to contribute greater diversity within an organized whole. The main consideration is that the diversity should be actually and effectually *organized*; it must not be mere multiplicity, but diversity within an organized whole.

THE INFLUENCE OF THE SPEAKER'S MANUSCRIPT

It is well known in a general way that the attention of the audience lags when the speaker confines himself closely to his notes or manuscript. But quantitative determination of the facts has not been often attempted. H. T. Moore [49] made a study of the impressiveness of a five-minute selection of the life and scientific work of Helmholtz, when this was presented in two ways. To one class the selection was read from notes. To another class, of presumably equal ability, the material was delivered in free utterance as a regular part of a lecture. Through pre-rehearsal the same tempo and intonation were preserved in the two cases.

When subsequently tested for their knowledge of this section of the material, it was found that the audience to whom the material had been freely delivered remembered 36 per cent more than did the audience to whom the material had been read from manuscript. Moore concludes, "This average difference of 36 per cent . . . seems to indicate that the disposition of an audience to give attention is one third greater for spoken utterance than for reading."

The data from the two classes are as follows:

Mode of Presentation	Average Score	Mean Variation	Cases
Reading from notes . .	26.9%	7.8%	69
Free utterance	36.7	8.5	31

Difference is 9.8%, which is 36% of the "reading" score.

Obviously there are all degrees of confinement to the manuscript. Moreover the manuscript exercises a more marked effect upon the speech and spontaneity of expression with some speakers than with others. The general question well merits more detailed experimental investigation, for the problem is more complex than these simple figures indicate. Inasmuch as brief reference to outline notes may well lend definiteness and coherence that might otherwise be absent, it would be interesting to know the quantitative effects of various degrees of reliance on notes. It would also be of interest to observe the degree to which speakers differ in the constraint exercised by the manuscript, as well as the particular manner in which this constraint operates.

Although we have spoken of attention, in the preceding sections, as the *first* task of the performer, it would of course be an error to suppose that this task, once accomplished, could then safely be forgotten. Over two thousand years ago Aristotle, in his *Treatise on Rhetoric*, remarked that in the case of the orator the audience might become less and less attentive as the discourse continued, and that although in the beginning the attention might be willingly given, toward the close special devices might be required to attract and hold it. In this respect, at least, audiences have not changed since the days of Aristotle. Our analysis of the performer-audience relation, therefore, must not be thought of as strictly mechanical. There is not only, on the whole, the actual *succession* of tasks, but also an *accumulation* of tasks as the performance proceeds. We must nevertheless speak of these tasks in succession, in the order of their initiation. From the practical point of view, what the performer has to bear in mind is that having once caught attention, he must continue to catch it; having once become interesting he must remain interesting.

PRACTICAL CONCLUSIONS

1. Attention once caught does not persist unless good grounds are provided for sustained interest; providing these grounds is the performer's second task.

2. Intrinsic interest of the subject matter is the most effective factor in sustaining attention; if this is lacking the only resort is to artificial devices.

3. The mechanical devices for sustaining attention are often irrelevant, weak, and transient; their value is greatest when the audience is immature, inexperienced, or of low intelligence.

4. *Rapport* of audience with performer is often secured by the latter's fortunate personal endowment; but it may be further promoted by preliminary preparation of the audience through the mode of announcement or through effective publicity.

5. At the time of appearance, *rapport* may be furthered by a variety of techniques—such as reference to topics of mutual concern, humorous remarks, complimentary statements or acts, dispelling the speaker's presumption of superiority; and by special ritual, regalia, or ceremony; music and especially some form of community activity, such as singing, are useful aids.

6. *Rapport* cannot be achieved by any kind of magic; nothing but light and sound pass between performer and audience; "psychic waves" of influence are just a figure of speech.

7. Make sure beforehand that distracting stimuli will not occur, or at least that they shall not occur at critical points in the performance, when intrusion would be most disastrous to *rapport* that has once been established.

8. Keep the exhibition, number, and arrangement of objects on the platform well within the average span of attention, but provide enough variety and clearness of organization so that shifting attention may still be directed favorably toward the region of the performance.

9. If speech is used, sentence length should not average over twenty-five words.

10. Free the discourse from notes or manuscript as fully as is consistent with fluent and easy delivery, for free utterance may be as much as a third more effective than reading closely confined to the manuscript.

11. Having caught attention and secured interest, do not fall back upon your oars; these two achievements must be carried on throughout the performance and sometimes special attention must be given to their deliberate revival.

CHAPTER VII

IMPRESSING THE AUDIENCE

THE BASIS OF IMPRESSION

In many cases the winning of an audience consists not merely of the immediate and transient effect upon them, but instead takes the form of conveying to each member a clear and definite impression which will abide with him and become a more or less permanent item of his knowledge. This is the third main task, that of impressing the audience with the speaker's theme or conclusions. It is of course a mistake to suppose that the impressiveness of the speaker comes solely from his speech. His personal appearance and manner, the mode in which his ideas are presented, the clearness and emphasis or force of his discourse, and the general setting and incidental associations of the occasion, all play their role. Not all of these lend themselves easily to measurement or experiment. One of the possible aids to impressiveness has however been submitted to scientific examination of at least a preliminary type,—*viz.*, the value of introducing visual and graphic material. Several studies have also been made of the relative impressiveness of visual and oral presentation, and of the impressiveness of the motion picture as compared with ordinary reading and oral narration.

VISUAL AND ORAL PRESENTATION

Simple and disconnected items, such as words or names, seem to be remembered better when seen than when heard. Kirkpatrick [36] arranged thirty names of

63

common objects in three columns of ten words each. The names in the first column were pronounced to pupils; those in the second column were written on the blackboard, uncovered one at a time, and erased; the objects corresponding to the names in the third column were also shown. His results are summarized in the following table.

Mode of Presentation of Ten Words	Averages for Boys and Girls	
	Immediate Memory	Memory after Three Days
Words spoken by teacher	7.1 words	1.0 words
Words seen on blackboard	7.2 "	2.0 "
Words spoken with objects seen . .	8.6 "	6.5 "

So far as immediate memory is concerned the three methods give much the same results, although the use or addition of visual elements gives a slight superiority. But from the point of view of permanence, or memory after the lapse of time, the methods are of very different value. Two of the seen words are recalled as compared with one of the heard words, on the average. But the most striking of all is the effect of presenting the visual object along with the spoken word. Memory for words thus presented is three to six times as effective as that for words merely seen or heard.

Pohlman [9] has reported a study of the memory of schoolchildren for materials presented in six different ways. The average per cent remembered, for each method, is given in the following table.

Mode of Presentation	Average Value
Objects presented and named	72%
Objects presented only	70
Names seen and heard	56
Names heard only	55
Names seen only	50
Names seen and spoken	49

The highest values are for the two series containing the objects themselves; next come the two series containing the hearing of the names; poorest of all are the two series in which the names were seen. Since each series was given but once, the accuracy of these results, taken alone, is open to question. However, it is only in the superiority of names heard over names seen that the results differ from those of Kirkpatrick.

T. V. Moore [50] conducted experiments on four adult subjects, presenting a series of objects, or pictures of objects, or written or spoken names of objects. After a series was presented, the subjects recalled all the items they could remember. They then busied themselves adding numbers, and at the end of one minute of work they were again asked to recall the series just shown them. About ten per cent more of the objects and pictures were remembered than of the written or spoken words. The average results are shown in the columns of the following table. A larger amount of that which was immediately remembered was also recalled after one minute in the case of pictures and objects.

MATERIALS PRESENTED IN THE ORIGINAL LIST	PER CENT OF TOTAL LIST IMMEDIATELY RECALLED	PER CENT OF ORIGINAL MEMORY RETAINED AFTER ONE MINUTE
Objects seen	88	97
Pictures seen	82	96
Written words seen	77	90
Spoken words heard	76	87

Moore also found in experiments on patients suffering from mental disorder that the inferior forms of memory suffered more than did the superior forms. In conclusion he writes: "If one attempts a day or a week later to recall a series, it is very rare that anything else than the real objects can be brought to mind. How clearly is

the value of object teaching impressed upon one's mind!
Certainly in any such subject as anatomy one should
never waste much time on the text. Never read a book if
you can look at a picture,—never be content with pictures if you can see a preparation."

Worcester [74] reported experiments on a group of adults,
to determine the relative ease of learning and the permanence of retention of 100-word prose passages (*a*) when
heard, and (*b*) when read. Neither method of presentation showed any advantage over the other either in time
required for original learning or in the number of repetitions required for this initial mastery.

But when the subjects were tested for accuracy of recall after periods of one, two, and seven days, the method
of auditory presentation was found to be unmistakably
superior. The following summary of the data will suggest the nature of the findings.

MEDIANS OF 13 SUBJECTS FOR	AVERAGE PER CENT ACCURACY AFTER		
	ONE DAY	TWO DAYS	SEVEN DAYS
Auditory presentation . .	81.4	83.0	75.0
Visual presentation . . .	73.6	76.0	67.2

Not only do these results come from the median values,
but for eleven subjects after one day and two days,
and for twelve subjects after seven days, the auditory
presentation was superior (there were thirteen subjects
in all). These results lead the investigator to conclude:

"In general it would appear that there is an intrinsic superiority for retention in the auditory method of presentation. If
this be so, it is of very great importance. It will mean, for
instance, that a teacher wishing children to memorize a poem,
will do better to read it aloud to them once a day, than to have
them read it to themselves once a day. It is probable also that
the lecture is more efficacious than the single reading of printed

matter, and still further, it implies that it is economical for two students to study orally together."

GRAPHIC AND VISUAL AIDS

Erickson and King [15] have made a comparison of visual and oral presentation in the case of pupils from the third to the ninth grades. "Two series of tests of four lessons each were given to the elementary classes in the following manner. The first section of each group studied a lesson from a book, which was presented orally by the teacher or the experimenter to the other section. They were told that they would be tested by questions after the presentation. Questions were immediately furnished each pupil on mimeographed sheets, the same set of questions for each section, and they were given all the time they desired to write the answers to them. The next day a second lesson was presented in the same way, except that the sections of each group which before read, now listened to the teacher or experimenter, and those which before listened, now read. This procedure was continued until each section had read two lessons which the other had listened to and had listened to two lessons which the others had read." The papers were scored on a percentage basis, and the results, for the different grades, with their different lessons are as follows:

GRADES	AVERAGE FOR READING	AVERAGE FOR ORAL PRESENTATION
3rd and 4th	52.5%	65.7%
5th and 6th	54.0	56.2
7th and 8th	62.6	65.0
9th	49.0	63.0
AVERAGES	54.5	62.5

The evidence here offered is clearly in favor of oral presentation and against mere reading, at least in the case of an audience of schoolchildren who are being given the subject matter of a lesson. Explanations will occur readily, but just as good explanations would have been suggested if the results had come out in favor of reading.

In another investigation, reported by Sumstine,[62] the question was raised, "Does a high-school pupil grasp and hold a subject better through the eye alone, or through the eye and ear combined, or through the ear alone?" A motion-picture film dealing with "farming with dynamite" was provided, accompanied by a lecture explaining the subject in detail. A series of questions served as an examination, to determine the amount and correctness of the information conveyed to high-school students who were presented with these materials in the following ways.

"The film was shown to one group. To another the film was shown and the accompanying lecture read. To the third group the teachers read the lecture. The pupils were asked to give their attention to an interesting story. Nothing was said about tests or the purpose of the story. Examinations were given at three different times, at the end of twenty-four hours, ten days, and three months. There were about 120 students in each group. Examination papers were rated on a percentile basis. A summary of the totals of all pupils for each group at the three test periods gives the following table:

PERIOD	FILM	FILM AND LECTURE	LECTURE
Twenty-four hours . . .	73.9%	70.8%	67.8%
Ten days	60.2	56.5	51.5
Three months	72.8	60.2	61.1

In all cases the results from the film alone are superior to either of the other methods, and except for the memory after three months, where there is no considerable difference, the results of film accompanied by lecture are superior to those of the lecture alone. It is of course unsafe to draw broad generalizations from a single experiment in which one film is compared with one lecture. This particular film may have been exceptionally impressive or this particular lecture may have been a poor one. But until these results have been contradicted by other measurements, they stand as extremely suggestive, and lead the investigators to remark that "Mental images received through the eye seem to be better remembered than images through the eye and ear or through the ear." And on the whole the lecture accompanied by the film gave better results or was more impressive than was the lecture alone.

But Lacy [38] has reported a somewhat similar investigation of the relative efficiency of three typical methods of presenting a story to 315 schoolboys from the seventh, eighth, and ninth grades. The three methods were (*1*) silent reading of a story by the pupils, (*2*) oral telling of the story to the pupils, and (*3*) presentation of the story to the pupils by means of a motion picture. The experiment was carefully planned, and leads the investigator to conclude that questions of fact, inference, or moral discrimination can be answered more adequately either in immediate or delayed recall when the narrative material has been presented by a story-teller or as reading matter than when presented through the motion picture. Of the two more successful methods of presentation, story-telling has the advantage.

However, after part of the story (*The Hoosier Schoolmaster*) had been presented to all the pupils by each of the three methods, "An opportunity was given for the subjects to vote upon the method by which they desired that the remaining two fifths of the story be presented, with the understanding that the preference thus expressed would be respected. As was to be expected the vote favored the presentation through the motion picture; next in order came the reading, while story-telling was the least popular of all. The percentages were respectively 90.8, 5.0, and 0.4, 3.8 not voting. Thus our results would indicate that the order of effectiveness of the various methods, where appeal to interest is concerned, is exactly the opposite of that which obtains if the ability to reproduce and apply the material is considered."

As a matter of fact, the average differences found by Lacy between the various methods were very small. In immediate recall, considering the final averages for all materials and all groups of students, oral presentation excelled reading by only 2 per cent and reading excelled the motion picture by 7 per cent. In the case of delayed recall after several weeks, the oral method excelled the reading by 3.6 per cent and the reading excelled the motion picture by less than one per cent. The results clearly contain nothing to discourage the speaker from the use of visual and graphic materials whenever these are convenient. Indeed, the investigator's own conclusions are sufficiently conservative. "The investigation, therefore, can make no claim to completeness, nor does it make possible a final estimate of the relative value of motion pictures as an educational agency. It may serve however to point out the advantage of methods already in vogue and serve as a warning against the assumption that motion pictures are unqualifiedly our most valuable educational agency."

Weber [69] performed a similar experiment on seventh-grade children. The experiments were carefully planned and conducted and comprehensively reported. In the first experiment a travelogue film was presented, and the information thus conveyed was tested by a Yes-No examination. Compared with this was the value of the oral presentation of the information, following in detail the various scenes of the film, and similarly tested. From a third group was secured a measure of "initial knowledge," before any presentation of such material. A fourth group had an oral presentation followed by the film. A fifth group was first shown the film and then given the oral description. The results were as follows, briefly:

1. Poorest of all was the oral presentation.
2. The film was superior to the oral presentation.
3. Next to film alone was oral followed by film presentation.
4. Best of all was film followed by oral presentation.
5. The film was voted to be more interesting than the narrative.

In another experiment the following were compared: (*a*) the motion-picture film alone; (*b*) oral presentation alone; (*c*) the film with accompanying remarks; (*d*) the study of a printed description. The subject of these presentations was geographical. Measured by the ability to give information verbally, there were no considerable differences between the methods. Measured by ability to draw the materials presented, the visual method was naturally the best, and it was also voted as being the most interesting.

The following diagram, adapted from Weber, portrays the relative effectiveness of three types of lesson presentation, with one variety of material, in the case of 300 seventh-grade schoolchildren, the same amount of time being given to each mode of presentation. The use of the film as an aid is seen to give greater effectiveness than the oral review in impressing knowledge, and the added

value is greater when the film precedes rather than follows the oral account.

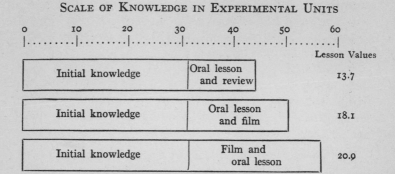

SCALE OF KNOWLEDGE IN EXPERIMENTAL UNITS

Initial knowledge	Oral lesson and review	13.7
Initial knowledge	Oral lesson and film	18.1
Initial knowledge	Film and oral lesson	20.9

In the above diagrams, "Initial knowledge" represents
that possessed by groups of individuals who were not
presented with any of the experimental accounts of the
subject matter. The added rectangles in each case represent the amounts of knowledge in excess of this exhibited by groups to whom special accounts of the subject
matter were presented in the various ways indicated.

Among various incidental results also suggested by
Weber's investigation are the following. They cannot of
course be completely generalized or held to hold on all
occasions, but they seemed to be clearly shown with the
materials, personnel, and circumstances of his experiments.

1. The visual aid (picture, diagram, film) more effectively
precedes than follows the oral exposition, especially if the subject matter be unfamiliar and the visual aid simpler and more
concrete than the oral presentation.

2. As the complexity or abstractness of the visual aid approaches that of the verbal account, in degree, the later in the
course of the exposition does it most effectively appear.

3. The visual aid is relatively more effective in the case of
observers of humble intelligence or immaturity than in the case

of those mentally more alert or more adult. The value of the visual aid increases with lack of experience on the part of the learners.

4. The value of the visual aid is shown in increased ability to remember material learned, as well as in the ease or adequacy of the initial learning.

5. Exhibiting the visual appeal does not necessarily effect learning and impression. Incidental learning is likely to be unreliable and weak. Hence the visual aid is most useful when the impression it gives is invigorated by oral discussion, question, or some active mode of expression.

The results of these various investigations may be brought together in the following rough outline fashion, for purposes of summary and comparison. First is given the name of the investigator; then follow in the order of relative effectiveness, by the methods employed, the various modes of presentation.

INVESTIGATOR	BEST METHOD	SECOND BEST	POOREST METHOD
Kirkpatrick	Objects seen and words heard	Words seen only	Words heard only
Pohlman	Objects seen only or with words heard	Words seen and heard, or heard	Words seen only
Moore	Objects or pictures seen	Words seen only	Words heard only
Erickson and King	Lesson heard only	....	Lesson seen (read)
Sumstine	Motion pictures seen only	Film seen and lecture heard	Lecture heard only
Lacy	Story heard only	Story seen (read)	Film seen only
Weber (1)	Film seen and story heard	Film seen only	Story heard only
Weber (2)	No considerable differences between film alone, story heard, film and story heard, or story read silently, except for ability to draw objects, in which the visual methods were superior.		
Worcester	Materials heard	....	Materials seen

These studies illustrate the numerous available ways of presenting material to an audience, and they suggest that the value of the various methods may depend on such facts as the nature of the material, the purpose of the presentation, the character of the audience, the method of measuring the results, the amount of interest aroused, and perhaps other undetermined factors. The different investigations are, as a matter of fact, far from comparable. Thus some of them employed disconnected words while others used meaningful material, such as prose passages. Nor can we compare words seen for two seconds with words spoken at the rate of one for each two-second period. And obviously the comparison of seen words with heard words is very different from the comparison of the seen pictures of objects with the heard names of them. But on no one type of comparison are there a sufficient number of investigations for us to be able to draw positive conclusions. In addition to these complications, results from children are not comparable nor combinable with those from adults. Furthermore, the detailed circumstances of each set of materials and type of experiment introduce complicating factors.

What some of these factors are is suggested by Gates [17] in the following words:

"Are children or adults so constituted by original nature that they acquire most readily reactions aroused by means of visual, or auditory, or tactual, or some other sensory stimulation? So far as we know, the primary and higher neural connections of the brain aroused through one sense organ are just as modifiable and retentive as are the centers stimulated by others. Other things being equal, we learn quite as readily through one sense as another, with the exception, of course, of individuals whose receiving connections or central mechanisms are defective. Other conditions, consequently, determine which avenue of presentation is to be preferred.

"Very young children learn new words better, for example, when presented to the ear than when presented to the eye, for the reason that their early word experience is auditory and not visual. If they have attended school, by the average age of eight or thereabouts children learn better by means of reading. The reasons, however, are not physiological but mechanical; the child can regulate the speed of reacting to the words to suit his capacity; he can attempt recall when and where he pleases; he can stop and repeat the especially difficult items, and disregard those already mastered.

"The relative value of moving pictures, graphs, diagrams, mechanical instruments, verbal explanations, and clay models are similarly determined by past experience and mechanical advantages. The main questions are: which method makes most clear the thing to be learned and which does it most interestingly and most economically of time, space, and money."

All these various investigations are about evenly divided on the question of the relative impressiveness of visual and auditory presentation of materials. But the evidence is fairly consistent in that the addition of visual materials to the auditory presentation is more favorable for memory than is auditory presentation alone. Remembering material is in large part a matter of organizing it. Visual presentation, added to the temporal flow of spoken words, enables spatial organization as well as organization in time. Where one form of organization fails or is difficult, the other supplements it or takes its place.

Moreover, the evidence is unanimous that the visually presented material is considered more interesting than is material orally presented. It is at least clear that the speaker who fails to take advantage of the interest and memory value of visual aids is ignoring some of the technique of impressiveness.

On the whole Lippman [41] is justified when he writes:

"Where action depends on whether a number of people are of one mind, it is presumably true that, in the first instance no idea is lucid for practical decision until it has visual or tactile value. . . . Pictures have always been the surest way of conveying an idea, and next in order, words that call up pictures in memory."

In a similar vein Kenagy and Yoakum [35] conclude:

"Most persons are *visual* minded. What they can see is much more easily understood and fixed in mind than what they hear or even read. Only when functions and relationships are pictured in chart form can every member of the organization clearly grasp the nature of his duties and his position in the organization."

INDIVIDUAL DIFFERENCES AND MODE OF PRESENTATION

One definite advantage of pictorial and graphic material over verbal presentation is based on the psychology of individual differences. In circumstances in which it is desired that all the members of a miscellaneous group derive approximately similar and uniform understanding of materials presented, this principle is important. Human beings differ from one another in numerous ways, and in some respects they are more diverse than in others.

Thus men are more alike in stature than in weight; more alike in size than in strength; more alike in simple, structural, and ancient traits than in complex, functional, and recently developed characteristics. They are more alike at rest than they are in action; more alike in appearance than in behavior. Men scarcely differ at all in the number and location of their fingers, but they vary enormously in the agility of these organs. Men are more alike in their needs and cravings than in the capacity to gratify these wants; more alike in their aims than in their ability to achieve these aims.

The greater the degree of symbolism entering into an activity, the more will individuals differ. Men are more alike in their ability to hear sounds and merely to see words than in their capacity to treat such sounds and shapes as signs and to comprehend their meanings. The more subtle the sign and the more abstract the meaning, the greater will be the diversities in understanding among the members of an audience. It is this point in particular that is related to mode of presentation.

The simplest modes of symbolism operate on the basis of *similarity*. The sign in some way and to greater or less degree resembles or is identical with the thing for which it stands. Actors on the stage *imitate* the persons and acts which they represent and thus symbolize. Pictures of things are more directly like the things they *represent* than are the words we use to describe them. Pictorial presentation is therefore less subtly symbolic than verbal narration or exposition, and motion pictures are still more closely related to the things they mean.

Somewhere between pictures and words, in this respect, come graphs, maps, diagrams, blueprints, and similar symbols. Rows of bricks are not represented by actual bricks, nor even by pictures of them, but by mere lines. But the lines run in the same directions as the rows of bricks, form similar angles; the marks on the map and blueprint sustain the same spatial relations as do the things for which they stand. But the subtler forms of symbolism rely on *contiguity* rather than on similarity. The word d-o-g, although it has neither tail nor legs, nevertheless *means* a quadruped. Its meaning is derived not from its resemblance to these animals, but from its association, through contiguity, with such creatures. Technical vocabulary and terminology show this situation even more strikingly. We can thus arrange the ways of telling a story in a scale of symbolism, in which in the beginning the symbolism is slight and based on similarity, increasing in subtlety, abstractness, and depen-

dence on sheer contiguity as the later steps on the scale
are reached. These steps would be as follows:

1. Seeing the actual events take place, or handling the concrete objects and materials.

2. Seeing the events "acted out," as in drama or pantomime,
by people who "represent" or symbolize the actual characters
and situations.

3. Motion-picture portrayal of the events, or of actions intended to represent them.

4. Photographs, still pictures of significant characters and
movements, or lantern slides of materials and objects.

5. Maps, diagrams, blueprints, and similar graphic repre-
sentations.

6. Verbal account and description, in the mother tongue,
using the vocabulary of daily life.

7. Description through the use of technical symbols and
terminology, a foreign speech, or similar sets of special and
recondite signs.

Now the earlier in this series or scale a method stands,
the more nearly alike will people be in their understanding of it, the more nearly uniformly and equally will they
be informed by its use. The later in the series or scale
the method stands, the greater will be the heterogeneity
of mankind in response to it, the more diverse the degrees
and modes of understanding. Furthermore, the earlier in
the scale the method stands, the more likely will be the
young, the dull, the ignorant, the uneducated, along with
the old, the bright, the sophisticated, to get the same
rudimentary meanings from it. Imbeciles and savants
get much the same comprehension from a representative
picture; but they differ strikingly in the use of the dic-
tionary or the encyclopedia. Idiots and infants understand gestures, but only in later development will the use
of linguistic signs of the verbal sort be possible.

In general then, if equal and universal understanding is sought for all the members of an audience, the earlier, more pictorial, and graphic methods of presentation will be found most dependable. The more heterogeneous the group composing the audience, the more useful will be these less highly symbolic methods in effecting a similar comprehension on the part of all the individuals, or on the part of the greater number. The younger, less sophisticated, and less educated the members of the group, also, the more effective will be the earlier methods in the scale, in promoting uniform understanding.

This general principle can often be put to good use in planning the presentation of materials and themes before mixed audiences, heterogeneous groups, assemblies of the whole staff of an organization. The more abstract and verbal modes of description or exposition can best be reserved for highly selected, more intelligent, and technically educated assemblages, the members of which are selected beforehand, on such grounds, as being at least more or less similar to one another. Concrete and pictorial presentation makes for uniformity of comprehension, even though the comprehension may not be profound. Verbal presentation makes for greater diversity of understanding. There are occasions in which it is the latter rather than the former that is desired,—where diversity of opinion, varieties of comprehension, are what is being sought. The mode of presentation should be adapted to the result that is to be accomplished.

If visual aids are to be used, it would be of interest to know something of the relative impressiveness and interest of the various available forms. Thus visual aids may take the form of tableau and pantomime, exhibition of objects, charts and graphs, pictures or lantern slides, as well as film and motion picture. Comparative studies in this field have also been made. Thus Revesz and Hazewinkel [56] presented material to groups of children, either by means of motion-picture film or through a comparable set of lantern slides. One week after the exposition, essays were called for reporting the material exhibited. Both for quantity and for accuracy of the reproduced material the lantern slides were superior. This superiority was the greater, the younger the children. Many variables enter into such a comparison, and it is probably not safe to make a broad generalization on the basis of any one investigation.

An experimental comparison of various modes of instruction has been reported by Freeman [16] and others with special reference to visual aids and their relative value. As illustrative of their findings Douglass [14] cites the following:

"McCluskey, in a carefully controlled experiment, found the film inferior to the oral and map method of teaching French explorations in United States history; the film inferior to the chalk talk in teaching about mountain glaciers; and the film inferior to the oral-chart method of teaching material concerning waste-disposal in cities. He found a stereopticon lecture more effective than the film in teaching the significance of the Panama Canal. He found oral instruction illustrated by stereopticon slides, and oral instruction illustrated by pictures and sketches, approximately equal to film instruction in dealing with the life history of the Monarch butterfly. He found stereographs slightly superior, and film much superior to slides in teaching matters concerning steamboats in United States history. James found the film superior to still pictures in teaching matter concerning Yellowstone Park, and lumbering in the north woods. The two McCluskeys found demonstration superior to the slide, the film, and the stereograph in teaching how to make a reed mat, the slide being the least effective in most instances. Rolfe found the demonstration clearly superior in teaching lessons on static electricity. Freeman, Shaw, and Walker found the film superior to the ordinary oral and demonstration methods of teaching handwriting.

"The general net result of the experiments conducted to determine the efficacy of the film, as compared with other types of visual aids, was stated by Freeman as follows: 'The comparison of the motion-picture film with other visual aids—slides, stereographs, still pictures—as means of informational instruction, indicates that the motion picture is superior within a restricted range of subjects' [as for example] 'where motion or action is among the essentials of the content to be learned.' "

A detailed and carefully controlled experiment has been reported by Tilton and Knowlton [63] on the effectiveness of using photoplay films for class instruction in history. The authors summarize the results in the following words:

"The films were used for 6 months in the history instruction of the 7th grade in six classes. Progress of the experimental group was compared with that made by a control group in the same school, also six classes, and taught by the same teachers. The experimental group was so selected that it was somewhat less able than the control group, so that any advantage shown by the experimental group could not be attributed to their higher intelligence.

"The films were used in the usual classrooms, during the regular history periods. Teachers used the same methods of instruction in both groups. The comparison was between ordinary classroom methods, filled with reading and discussion, and classroom procedures in which one-fifth of the periods were occupied with viewing the films, the rest of the periods being used in the regular way.

"The pupils who saw the films learned 19 per cent more and retained 12 per cent more than the others. The use of the films was so effective that children of average ability, using the films, learned as much as much more intelligent pupils without their use. Those using the films also participated more freely in the voluntary discussion, about 10 per cent oftener, and they read about 40 per cent more in the supplementary reading assignments."

The details of this elaborate experiment are too minute and complicated for discussion here, but the net conclusions drawn were:

1. The photoplays contributed materially to the gaining and retention of worth-while knowledge, particularly of knowledge of interrelationships, other than those of time.

2. They produced more pupil participation in classroom discussion.

3. They caused the pupils who saw them to read voluntarily more supplementary history reading material under controlled classroom conditions.

RELATIVE MERITS OF GRAPHIC PRESENTATIONS

Studies have also been made of the relative merits and impressiveness of various ways of presenting data in graphic form. Various tabular, graphic, and textual arrangements may differ in the intelligibility which they give to such quantitative data as those concerning population, historical statistics, earnings, imports, and the like. And the method most suitable for one kind of material may not be the best for other kinds of data.

Washburne [67] has conducted experiments on several thousand junior high-school students, endeavoring to secure "objective measurement of the effect . . . of various arrangements of quantitative material." The procedure was as follows:

"A short account of the economic history of Florence was written. This unit was selected in order that the content might be equally unfamiliar to all the children. The narrative included one paragraph which contained specific quantitative facts. In each of the forms (of which there were 14 or 15) this paragraph was varied. The rest of the material was constant; and the paragraph varied only in the *form of presentation*, not in the data themselves.

"Between 200 and 300 pupils were tested on each form. In some of the forms the quantitative paragraph appeared as a statistical table, in others as a bar-graph, in others as a pictograph or a line-graph, and in still others the data were given in narrative form."

Examinations were given in all cases, covering the data presented in the complete account, and scores secured for the correctness with which each question was answered, and the various forms thus compared in their effectiveness. These questions fell into three groups, according to the nature of the facts concerning which they inquired. These groups were as follows:

A. Questions dealing with *specific amounts*; as, "How much did the wool merchants earn in the year 1100?"

B. Questions dealing with *static comparisons*; as, "Who earned the most in the year 1100, the wool, silk, or Calimala merchants?"

C. Questions concerning *dynamic comparisons*; as, "Between the years 1100 and 1438 whose earnings increased most rapidly, those of the wool, silk, or Calimala merchants?"

Among the conclusions suggested on the basis of this investigation, the following are of interest in the present connection. Numerous other comparisons are to be found discussed in the original article.

I. For complex or slightly complex static comparisons, use a bar graph.
II. For extremely simple static comparisons use a pictograph.
III. For dynamic comparisons use a line graph.
IV. For specific amounts use a statistical table.

V. For specific amounts use round numbers in numerical form (*e.g.*, 5,000, not 5,622, nor five thousand).

VI. For specific amounts use as few facts as possible.

VII. Never present numerical data in textual (paragraph) form if there are more than one or two items to be presented.

VIII. When numerical data are presented textually, use written numbers (*e.g.*, five thousand dollars) for static and dynamic comparisons, and numerals (*e.g.*, $5,000) for specific amounts.

IX. Use questions after a graph to emphasize its chief features.

The following groups show the samples from Washburne of the various ways used to show quantitative data.

1. Paragraph

The income of the leading Calimala merchants grew very much between 1100 and 1438. In 1100 their income probably did not amount to more than $5,000 (estimated in U. S. money). But in 1438 they earned more than $10,000,000. The income of the wool manufacturers grew almost as rapidly (although it was not as large) as that of the Calimala merchants. In the year 1100 the wool manufacturers earned a little over $1,000,000. In 1438 they earned about $7,000,000. The income of the silk merchants (though much smaller) also grew; in 1100 it was only about $2,000 while in 1438 it was over $2,000,000.

2. The Statistical Table

Year	Calimala Merchant's Income Estimated in U. S. Money	Wool Manufacturer's Income Estimated in U. S. Money	Silk Merchant's Income Estimated in U. S. Money
1100	$5,000	$1,000,000	$2,000
1175	3,000,000	2,000,000	100,000
1250	4,000,000	3,000,000	200,000
1358	7,000,000	5,000,000	600,000
1438	10,000,000	7,000,000	2,000,000

3. THE BAR GRAPH

Guild	Income Estimated in U. S. Money	Year
	2,000	1100
Silk	100,000	1175
	2,000,000	1438
	1,000,000	1100
Wool	2,000,000	1175
	7,000,000	1438
	5,000	1100
Calimala	3,000,000	1175
	10,000,000	1438

4. THE PICTOGRAPH

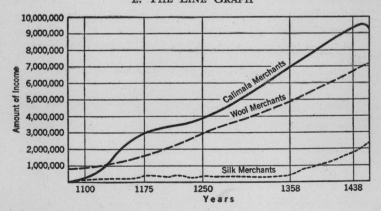

E. THE LINE GRAPH

MODES OF EMPHASIS IN PUBLIC SPEAKING

The problem of being impressive is in part that of being emphatic. The item that impresses us, in the sense that it catches our attention, is likely also to impress us, in the sense of sticking in our memory. Psychologists express this general fact by saying that vividness adds to memory value, and vividness is some sort of emphasis. Now the public speaker has a notion of the relative importance of the various statements he is about to make, before he utters them. The mere content of his statements may not immediately inform his auditors of the relative importance of these statements in the mind of the speaker.

Suppose then that the speaker desires to hint immediately at what he considers the relative importance of his statements to be, and wishes to stress some of these so that they will have high memory value because of this emphasis. How shall he proceed? How can the speaker add emphasis to a statement in addition to that which its content or meaning gives it in the mind of his auditors? Shall he bang his fist on the table, assert the proposition in an unusually loud shout, pause impressively before making the remark, reiterate the statement, speak it with remarkable slowness, accompany it by gesture, or verbally inform the audience that he is now about to say something of great importance? If reiteration, for example, is to be used, how many shall the repetitions be, and where shall they best occur in the discourse?

The most relevant study of the techniques of emphasis in presenting spoken material to an audience is reported by Jersild.[31] This investigator began by setting a series of problems for himself, in the following words:

"The public lecturer who aims to effect a careful balance of emphasis within the substance of his address might profitably raise the following questions: What point in a discourse is the most impressive, the beginning, the middle, or the end? What is the effect of repeating a statement one or more times, and how can this repetition be accomplished to the best advantage? What is the value of emphasis devices ordinarily used in public speaking? And finally, how do various degrees and forms of these factors compare with one another in strength?"

A biographical sketch of a fictitious person, containing seventy statements, was prepared, and after preliminary rehearsal by the speaker, presented to ten different audiences, with subsequent tests of what each person remembered of the discourse. Various propositions were emphasized, in different ways, and by ingenious methods it was arranged that different propositions should be emphasized in a given way before each audience, thus giving ten measures, using different statements, of each method of emphasis, and average results with a high degree of validity. The modes of emphasis experimented with were the following, the figures giving the relative values, when an unemphasized statement, occurring in the middle of the discourse, is taken as the basis of comparison, or 100 per cent. The methods are here arranged in decreasing order of effectiveness.

MODE OF EMPHASIS

	VALUE
5 repetitions, distributed at different points through the discourse	315
4 distributed repetitions of a statement	246
3 distributed repetitions	197
Verbal emphasis, "Now, get this," prior to making the statement	191
Primacy—the first statement of the 70	175
2 distributed repetitions (statements 11 and 60)	167
Primacy—second statement of the discourse	163
2 distributed repetitions (statements 35 and 40)	162
Verbal emphasis, "Did you get that?" after making the statement	154
Pause, before making the statement, for a time equal to that required to make a statement	143
2 repetitions in immediate succession, toward end of discourse (statement 60)	139

These various modes of emphasis were chosen to represent the usual array of techniques actually in common use by public speakers. Their relative measures do not of course show to what extent they affect the animation of the discourse as a whole, but they do demonstrate in a very neat manner their value in emphasizing the points they were meant to emphasize. Numerous interesting comparisons are made possible by this table of relative experimental values. The results are summarized by the investigator in the following words:

"The most effective, though not the most economical, form of emphasis is repetition to the extent of three or more presentations. The benefit arising from repetition does not increase in proportion to the number of added repetitions.

"Repetition is most effective when the several presentations are separated by intervals of time. One of the least effective forms of emphasis is to repeat an item immediately following its first presentation.

"The most impressive point in a discourse is the opening statement. The first statements have a distinct advantage over those which come last. To surpass the effect of primacy it is necessary to resort to three or more repetitions or to introduce special verbal emphasis devices.

"Of the more artificial forms of emphasis, the device of using verbal comments which direct attention to an item is

most effective. Next in effectiveness comes the device of introducing a short pause; following this, that of raising the voice
above the accustomed amplitude; gesticulation, by a gesture
and banging with one's fist, comes next in order, and in general has a beneficial effect. The device of speaking very slowly
not only stands lowest in effectiveness but has a decided negative effect."

Early assertion, verbal direction of attention to the
statement just made or about to be made, and reiteration are the devices which the experiment shows to be the
most effective modes of emphasis. It is interesting, however, to note that reiteration has its limits, and these
limits seem to follow the same law that is disclosed in
most studies of memory and attention,—the "law of
diminishing returns." Two assertions are not twice as
effective as one; instead they are only about 1.6 times as
effective. Four assertions are only a bit over twice as
effective as one. Roughly speaking the data suggest that
the effect of reiteration increased only approximately as
the square root of the number of repetitions. If this law
holds generally, sixteen repetitions would be only about
twice as effective as four, and they might also become
otherwise obnoxious. Primacy is of course a factor of
which the speaker can take but one advantage, although
the emphasis given by the "pause" perhaps operates by
giving the effect of "starting over," and thus securing
another use of primacy. Verbally calling attention to
one's statements must also have its practical limitations,
which good sense should restrain the speaker from
exceeding.

MODES OF READING AND SPEAKING

Interesting experiments have been reported by Woolbert [73] who sought to measure the influence, on the impressiveness of public reading, resulting from changes of

various types in the manner of reading. Stories were read to small audiences by a trained reader, who, on a given occasion, would adopt a particular mode of reading throughout the performance. Tests of impressiveness were then made by measuring the correctness of memory for the facts of the story after the lapse of five days.

The attributes of sound are pitch, intensity, time, and quality. Ordinary speech involves changes in all these to a greater or less degree. Suppose now that the speaker introduces wider ranges of pitch than usual, his voice thus rising to a higher pitch and falling to a lower pitch than is customary, either in sliding within the single syllable or in stepping from one syllable to the next. What effect does the increased amount of *pitch change* have on the impressiveness of his words, providing that the other attributes do not change beyond their usual or median amount?

Ten subjects were used in various experiments of this type, and although different individuals vary somewhat in the matter, we may take the average of the ten subjects when unadapted to the experiment as indicating the most probable tendency in the case of unprepared audiences. Most effective or impressive of all were two types of change,—the one being *extreme change of quality,* and the other *extreme change of all four attributes.*

Extreme change of quality is described as "carrying the virtue of interestingness"; it gives the effect of a continuing change of emotion; and it is produced by "placing the voice so that there is continual change in the various resonance-producing chambers of the head, throat, and chest."

The latter mode, in which every kind of change is used in profusion, with extreme variation its chief characteristic, is described as being "the mode that would be judged effective in making commonplace statements interesting and easy to listen to."

Least impressive of all the eleven modes of speaking adopted was that in which there was *no change whatever* in any of the four attributes, thus giving the extreme of monotony and complete uniformity of pitch, intensity, time, and quality. The listeners have difficulty in catching the words and in apprehending their logical meaning.

Four modes of speaking were found to possess no more than average impressiveness. These were median change of all four attributes, giving the general "effect produced by a congregation reading a Psalm in unison" and lacking brightness and animation; no change of pitch, with median change in the other three attributes, a mode resembling "the 'intoning' customs used by certain ecclesiastical sects"; extreme change of intensity, with median change of the other three, which mode, it is said, seems to benumb the listeners; and no change of quality, with median change of the other three attributes, a mode that is said to "make the reader appear sick or weak."

Except for the two modes first described, only four modes gave better than this average impressiveness. These were extreme change of pitch; no change of time, with resulting staccato effect; extreme change of time in the pauses between syllables, words, phrases, sentences, and other units, giving an animated effect; and no change in intensity, which gave the impression that the speaker was tired and uninterested.

Perhaps the safest conclusion suggested by these confessedly preliminary experiments is the author's, that, "There is a presumption in favor of using an extreme degree of change in all four attributes of sound during speech, especially for the purpose of securing retentiveness over an extended time."

Subsidiary conclusions drawn are that for intellectual impressiveness as thus measured: A wide range of pitch is preferable to no change; an even rate is superior to a rate excessively broken; interference with normal degree of change in intensity and elimination of changes in quality produce inferior results.

Woolbert's experimental data are summarized in the following table, derived from his report and somewhat rearranged, so as to give the changes in the approximate order of their impressiveness.

MODE OF READING	AVERAGE OF TEN CASES		
Attributes P = Pitch I = Intensity T = Time Q = Quality	Per Cent of Complete Memory Five Days after the Reading of the Stories		
	Unadapted Subjects	Adapted Subjects	Average
1. Extreme change of all four attributes	.70	.61	.66
2. Extreme change of Q., others median	.70		
3. No change of T., others median . .	.60	.69	.65
4. Extreme change of T., others median	.61	.48	.54
5. Extreme change of P., others median	.58	.49	.54
6. Median change of all attributes . .	.45	.61	.53
7. No change of I., others median . .	.54	.45	.50
8. No change of P., others median . .	.39	.58	.49
9. Extreme change of I., others median	.47	.43	.45
10. No change of Q., others median . .	.43		
11. No change of any of the four attributes	.28	.41	.34

If we take the average result of his listeners, both the unadapted and the adapted, for those modes for which both sets of data are given, we should conclude that only two modes are superior (of those given, which omit all quality changes). These would be the staccato effect produced by no change of time (duration of pauses), and extreme change of all attributes. Poorest of all still remains "no change of any of the attributes."

Inasmuch as "extreme change of quality" gives the same measure of impressiveness as is given by "extreme change of all attributes," it may be well to describe, in the author's own words, the mode of speech thus characterized.

"Changes in quality (timbre) are least common of all. Changes of quality are probably more influential than any other type of change in revealing the emotional state of the speaker. Emotional states involve muscular and vascular changes in the throat and pharynx, and thus the body of overtones is greatly affected in number and intensity, producing attention changes in quality.

"In this mode (extreme change of quality, median change of the other three) various complexities of tone are produced by 'placing' the voice so that there is a continual change in the various resonance-producing chambers of the head, throat and chest. The effect is what is loosely called a continuing change of 'emotional' tone. This makes it a rather common manner of speaking. It carries the virtue of 'interestingness.'

"Changes in quality are commonly assumed to represent changes in emotion, mood, total attitude, and hence to be highly impressive. This study strongly confirms this judgment."

Sarah Bernhardt, in her notes on "The Art of Acting," writes in a similar fashion, in the following words:

"The voice is the most important of all the actor's possessions. By means of the voice the attention of the public is riveted; the voice it is which binds together actor and auditor. An actor's voice must run the whole gamut of harmonies— grave, plaintive, vibrating, metallic."

A study such as that reported by Woolbert is interesting because it shows that the vocal attributes are important not only in the immediate speaker-audience relation, but have a further relation to the final retention and impressiveness of what is presented. This is a type of influence which only the experimental method could disclose, inasmuch as ordinary observation affords neither comparative measures nor standards of comparison.

In radio broadcasting the practice is often adopted of introducing dialogue in the less interesting descriptions and advertising announcements. The added interest and animation thus secured are in part due to the variety of voice changes when different speakers utter successive sentences.

A study by Buehler [8] of the modes of creating atmosphere by various techniques in addressing an audience has been reported but not published in detail.

The speaker attempted to express to the audience certain emotions "by voice only," "by action only," and "by combination of voice and action." Extraneous factors which might also determine atmosphere were so far as possible eliminated, "such as physical setting, meaning and emotion, language, and in some cases stage presence." Thus the letters of the alphabet were used instead of meaningful words, so as to eliminate moods connected with special topics of discourse. The chief results are reported to be the following:

"1. The tone quality of the reader's voice is a most important factor in affecting the emotional tone of an audience. The audience is stirred more by the auditory impressions which it receives from the reader than by the visual impressions. The response in the audience tends to be largely emotional.

"2. The expression of the emotions through the symbol of action enables the audience to identify the emotion he is expressing; they are more intelligible to the audience. The response in the audience tends to be largely intellectual. The audience is moved by what it hears and understands more than by what it sees."

These conclusions cannot of course be too hastily extended beyond the situations actually experimented with.

They do not, for example, show that an audience will be more profoundly moved by an oral narration of an action than by a motion-picture portrayal of the deed. But there is no doubt that words have a power peculiar to themselves. Not only do they arouse the cognitive understanding of the meanings they imply, but vocal sounds, by their intimate association with emotional conditions, tend directly to arouse appropriate emotions through their vocal properties alone, in addition to such communication of descriptive meanings as they are used for in the calm narration of facts.

Weaver [68] tried to discover a team of tests which might enable the detection beforehand of those individuals who possessed the aptitude for effective public vocal expression (interpretative). He had 210 college students (men) read a selection before audiences. Each member of the audience rated each performer for the effectiveness of his vocal expression.

The investigator then applied intelligence tests and the array of Seashore measures of musical talent. Believing that talent for vocal impression might be analyzed into general intelligence, emotional responsiveness, neuro-muscular co-ordination, and audition, he sought to measure two of these factors and to correlate them with the estimate of effectiveness as judged by actual auditors. In the final cases, a simple vocabulary test was used as the intelligence measure. The following correlations were found between "vocal expression" and the other features:

Sense of pitch correlated with vocal expression . . . +.48
Sense of intensity correlated with vocal expression . . +.18
Sense of time correlated with vocal expression . . . +.19
Sense of consonance correlated with vocal expression . +.32
Tonal memory correlated with vocal expression . . . +.35
Vocabulary intelligence correlated with vocal expression . +.27

By refined methods of multiple and partial correlation, this team of tests was made to correlate by a maximum figure of $+.52$ with vocal expression (sense of consonance was eliminated from the final team). The most striking feature of the results seems to be the fairly significant relation between sensitiveness of the ear to pitch and skill in using the voice expressively.

While this investigation cannot be said to have produced a method of identifying an individual's future skill as a public speaker, it perhaps points the way to the discovery of those special endowments which make this skill possible. Sense of pitch, for example, is said to be a function that is not capable of improvement through practice, but represents a native trait.

CLIMAX AND ANTICLIMAX

Under the heading of Impressiveness we may consider the effectiveness of different methods of presenting material of a graphic or printed sort as well. Thus a series of points may be arranged in the order of *climax* or in the order of *anticlimax*. In the first case the less imposing details are placed at the beginning and the more imposing details follow in order of their importance, concluding with the most imposing. The anticlimax order reverses this arrangement. Is one arrangement more impressive than the other?

Experimental data on this point are limited to a single investigation by Adams,[1] who used printed material in the form of advertisements, presented in dummies to 463 subjects, the whole series, in a given dummy, being seen at a single sitting. Subsequent tests for memory of the advertisements seen were used to give a measure of the impressiveness of the two arrangements.

A given firm was represented in the dummy by four

advertisements, distributed through the total group. These advertisements of a given firm varied in size from quarter to full page. The smaller sizes might be presented first, followed by the larger, thus giving the climax order, or the reverse order would give the anticlimax. Combining the results for many firms for each type of arrangement and for all the subjects gives average results on the basis of which a comparison may be made.

In the following table which is derived from the data presented by Adams, Q, H, and F stand for quarter, half, and full pages. The average value for the climax order is in each case taken as 100 per cent and the anticlimax order value stated on this base. The table gives the results for various sizes and arrangements.

Sizes and Their Arrangement	Climax Order Average Value	Anticlimax Order Average Value
F F F H	100	109.2
F F F Q	100	100.5
F F H H	100	101.4
F F Q Q	100	125.8
F F H Q	100	113.9
F H H H	100	99.4
F Q Q Q	100	112.3
F H H Q	100	111.3
F H Q Q	100	110.1
H H H Q	100	116.9
H H Q Q	100	91.3
H Q Q Q	100	128.1
Averages	100	110.0

So far as these results indicate, the anticlimax order makes a somewhat deeper impression than does the climax order, the average advantage amounting to ten per cent. We cannot of course generalize this finding without further data. The investigation was limited to printed appeals, their relative imposingness depended solely on their relative magnitude, and impressiveness was measured only by a particular memory test. The results have nevertheless a suggestive value as following from an attempt to put to experimental test definite problems in the psychology of appeal. They are moreover supported by certain practical sales manuals which urge the salesman not to rely on climax order but to "present the best arguments first."

Thus in the latest sales manual distributed to its salesmen, a progressive manufacturing concern issues such advice as the following:

"Usually it is best to start with the most striking features rather than work up to a climax. Here is one point in which the study of the psychology of the buyer yields a valuable suggestion. For many reasons the first minutes of the sales interview count the most, and the effort of the salesman should be directed to using them to the best possible advantage."

In another connection a special section of advice is given, under the heading "The Best Selling Points Should be Presented First." Here it is urged that:

"Another point of almost equal importance is that the strongest arguments, as the salesman judges the prospect to see them, should be presented first. . . . It is of course recognized that the salesman often requires a little time to 'size up' his man, but it should always be his aim to keep this preliminary period to a minimum and to advance his strongest arguments at the earliest possible moment."

It seems clear at least that the value and effectiveness of climax from the point of view of final impressiveness merits further investigation. It is entirely possible that the traditional attitude toward the climax order was determined by the amount of "excitement" caused by it, rather than by any question of permanence of impression. It may even be that climax is often resorted to only because interest is likely to wane during the course of an ordinary presentation, and climax is required to keep it up to its original intensity. Experimental studies are needed on the various types of climax order, and on the effect produced by them.

IMPRESSIVENESS AND TEMPORAL ORDER

That the impressiveness of arguments or pieces of evidence depends in part upon the order of their presentation has been shown by Lund [42] in a series of experiments upon this point. His subjects had already rated, for belief strength, different propositions with which he worked. For this part of the experiment, propositions were chosen which showed only a moderate degree of belief, when presented without argument or evidence. They might thus be shifted either higher or lower on the belief scale as the result of data or discussion.

Two printed arguments or discussions were now prepared for each proposition. The one argument was on the affirmative, the other on the negative side, of a given proposition. To one group of subjects the affirmative argument was first presented, after which the propositions were rated for belief strength. Subsequently the negative discussion was presented, and the propositions subsequently rated again for belief strength. To another group of subjects the arguments or discussions were presented in the reverse order,—first the argument for the negative, then that for the affirmative. After each, the propositions were rated by each individual. All ratings were done without reference to previous ratings, and adequate time intervals intervened between different parts of the experiment.

The influence of the arguments is disclosed by the amount of deflection in the belief ratings produced by them. Both types of discussion produced definite and measurable deflections in belief. But the most striking fact revealed was that the *first* argument presented, whether affirmative or negative, was much more influential than the later one. Impressiveness is thus seen to depend in part upon temporal order. In discussing his results, Lund makes the following applications.

"A belief may gain a personal connotation though it has never been expressed. To have formed an opinion and inwardly to have yielded to its persuasive influence is sufficient to make it seem *ours* and something to which we owe allegiance. The significance which these facts give to primacy as an important constituent in belief and persuasion has certain practical bearings, some of which may be enumerated.

"A. The speaker or writer engaged in a debate or dealing with a controversial subject, in observing the importance of primacy, should not follow the climax order in presenting his argument, but should weaken sympathy with his opponent promptly by attacking his strongest argument first, thus lessening the force of his adversary's case as quickly as possible.

"B. In a debate, other things being equal, the affirmative, or whatever side of the question is first presented should have the advantage according to the influence of primacy. However in staged debates the principle is likely to be much less influential because of the more objective attitude taken by the audience toward the issue itself.

"C. The advertiser interested in presenting a series of advertisements, which differ in magnitude or attention value, should get the best results by observing the anticlimax order.

"D. Whether we are democrats or republicans, protestants or catholics, is frequently observed to be a consequence of paternal or ancestral affiliation. However, it is doubtful whether family ties or family considerations are nearly as important determinants as the fact that we *first* become familiar with the beliefs and the defenses of our family.

"E. Our form of jury trial, just as our procedure in debates, assumes that both sides are given an equal opportunity. But the existence of such equality is based on logical considerations, and assumes that logical factors will control the decision of the judges or jurymen as the case might be. But our beliefs are rarely if ever fashioned through such dispassionate weighing of pros and cons. While the lawyer of the plaintiff is reviewing his case and making his appeal, the belief of the jurors is already in the process of formation, and they are not to be dissuaded from their position by an equal amount of evidence or persuasive appeal on the part of the defendant's lawyer, according to the law of primacy, which appears as an indubitable factor in persuasion."

Adams's results, showing the superiority of the anti-climax order for the impressiveness of printed appeals, and Lund's results, showing the extreme importance of priority in persuasion, have a special interest in connection with the psychology of the audience. This arises from the fact that both sets of results contrast rather definitely with the conventional arrangement of programs and the time-honored organization of a theme. Traditionally the climax order is supposed to have a unique effectiveness. Thus such instructions as the following are commonly given to those preparing addresses and orations, as well as compositions to be read rather than heard:

"The several divisions must follow one another progressively, each growing out of its predecessor, so that the entire series may move toward a climax." (Esenwein, *How to Attract and Hold an Audience*, p. 108.)

"Climax is a most valuable means of emphasis. When three clauses of similar form are used together they make a strong impression. This is especially true if they follow Herd's principle of having the shortest first and the longest last." (Hotchkiss, *et al., Principles of Advertising*, p. 180.)

In general, the whole question of the effectiveness of the climax organization merits more detailed experimental study. And this is but one illustration of a great number of traditional principles which have been more or less generally accepted on the basis of authoritative assertion or convention. All these principles should be re-examined in the light of experimentally established evidence.

The circumstances of the occasion may have much to do with the relative values of climax and anticlimax order. Thus the occasion of a hurried sales interview with a busy and impatient executive probably introduces determinants not present in the case of the more leisurely relationship of speaker and ordinary audience. And the oral presentation, which is temporarily fixed in its sequences, may differ from the printed appeal, which is more objectively capable of review and back reference by the reader. Indeed, time limits may in themselves be important, so that the value of climax order in the brief presentation may be different from that in the more prolonged argument.

THE FORGETFULNESS OF AN AUDIENCE

For speakers interested in the permanent impression of an audience, it is important to know something concerning the tendencies to forgetfulness and the factors that increase the retention of presented materials and facts. Definite studies of these points have been made by Jones [33] in the case of typical audiences of college students.

Over a long period of time, and with various classes, measures were secured by systematic quizzes at the end of forty-minute lectures on general psychology, of the amount of the lecture material retained by the auditors

at the end of the lecture. Thirty lectures were studied
in the case of one performer, and in the case of another,
specially chosen for experiment because of recognized
exceptional talent as a lecturer, twelve lectures were
measured. The results showed that 60 per cent to 70 per
cent of the lecture points could be given from immediate
memory, at the close of the hour, the average being 62
per cent.

Studies were also made of the amount remembered
after the lapse of varying time intervals. Three or four
days after the typical lecture the audience remembered
about 50 per cent of it; after a week, about 37 per cent;
after two weeks, 30 per cent; and after eight weeks, 23
per cent. The curve of forgetting is similar to that found
for all sorts of memory, falling rapidly at first and then
slowly. Using the total amount of the lecture as the base
of comparison, we can say that 38 per cent is forgotten
at once; 12 per cent more during the ensuing three or
four days; and by the end of the first week a total of
63 per cent is gone. During the second week 7 per cent
more will be lost; during the next six weeks only about
1 per cent a week will be lost. The 23 per cent retained
by the end of that time will disappear very slowly, some
of it perhaps lasting for a lifetime.

Any device that will increase the immediate memory
of the audience, and any method that will prevent the
speedy rate of forgetting, will be a useful bit of technique, when permanent impression is sought. Of course,
various kinds of vividness, as well as repetition, concrete
application, and other modes of re-enforcement, may be
relied on, and usually are to an extent limited only by
the zeal and ingenuity of the performer.

Jones experimented with the device of giving a brief
and summary but fairly complete review examination

during the closing minutes of his lecture hour. Classes to whom these review tests were given were compared with those with whom the device was not employed. It was found that the memory was fully 50 per cent better, for intervals ranging from three days to eight weeks, in the case of audiences with which the immediate test device was used. The best time at which to give such a summary review test was immediately after the close of the lecture.

Obviously for many types of audience this examination device, with its striking effects on retention of material presented, cannot be employed. The principle underlying the result is chiefly that the auditors actively exercise, in the written review, just those connections and expressions which will be needed at the end of the memory interval. For audiences of the school or college type, for informational lectures, for instructional sessions of employees, operators, salesmen, and the like, the speaker can profitably employ some such additional technique of impression.

THE RATE AT WHICH AN AUDIENCE FORGETS A LECTURE

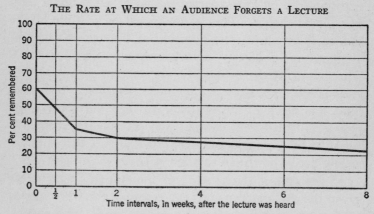

The above graph represents the results of Jones's experiments on the rate at which an audience of college students forgot the subject matter of lectures on psychological topics. Tests for knowledge were given at different periods of time after the hearing of the lecture. The following table, adapted from the account given by Jones, shows the actual figures, in per cent retained, the time intervals, the number of lectures used in securing the averages, the number of individuals whose records were used, and the probable error of the corrected coefficients of memory.

Delay Interval	No. of Lectures	No. of Cases	Corrected Memory Values	Probable Errors
Immediate . .	30	782	62.0	0.7
3–4 Days. . .	15	422	49.8	2.0
1 Week . . .	4	111	36.7	1.4
2 Weeks . . .	5	101	30.0	1.5
8 Weeks . . .	3	69	23.1	1.5

A very similar curve of forgetting is found for information acquired over a larger period of time, rather than in a single sitting. This is illustrated by a study of the loss of information over a period of time on the part of students in a botany course, reported by Johnson.[32] Through a study of earlier classes, an objective and scaled subject-matter examination had been prepared. This was given to the students on their entrance to the course (a three-term course) and the median score was found to be 5.5 points out of a possible 298, that is, practically zero knowledge to start with.

At the end of the course, all the students were again given the examination. As the result of the work during the course and the general preparation for this examination, the median score was found to be 205 points, immediately after completing the course. Subsequently different groups of the students, of the same average intelligence, were again given the examination, after 3 months, 15 months, and 27 months, respectively. The scores were, for these three groups, 110 points, 53 points, and 49 points.

That is, in the first three months, 46 per cent or nearly one half of the knowledge had been lost; a year later (15 months after the course closed) 74 per cent had been lost. But that retained up to this time was fairly permanent; after the lapse of another year only 2 per cent more (76 per cent in all) had been lost. Roughly speaking, after a lapse of two years students, who have meanwhile been continuing in school work of various kinds, retain only 24 per cent of the knowledge acquired through three terms of work in botany.

PRACTICAL CONCLUSIONS

1. Visual combined with auditory presentation of material is often more impressive than either alone.

2. Diagrams, pictures, and other visual aids are more effective when they precede than when they follow oral exposition, especially if they are simple and the subject matter unfamiliar.

3. Visual aids to oral presentation are of greater value with audiences of humble intelligence, immaturity, or inexperience.

4. The relative value of visual and oral presentation, if one only can be used, is not always the same; it varies with other variables.

5. Important variables in this connection are the nature of the material, the purpose of presentation, the intelligence, habits, and character of the audience, the method of determining the results, and the costs in time and apparatus.

6. Most persons are visual minded; they more easily grasp and better remember what they see than what they hear.

7. The more concrete the materials presented, the more

uniformly will all the members of the audience be impressed by it.

8. Similarity symbols, such as pictures and diagrams, are more easily and uniformly comprehended than are symbols such as words and formulae, based on contiguity.

9. The more technical and abstract the symbols used, the greater will be the diversity of effect on different observers.

10. Not all graphic devices are equally intelligible nor easily remembered; the detailed rules for graphic presentation should be carefully regarded.

11. The audience appears to be more moved by what it hears but more permanently impressed by what it sees.

12. In public speaking that use of the voice is most impressive which utilizes extreme changes of tone quality, or of all the attributes of sound.

13. Among the special devices usable in oral delivery by way of emphasis, the most effective, though not the most economical, is repetition, to the extent of three or more assertions.

14. The effect of repetition follows a law of diminishing returns.

15. Repetitions are most effective when they are spaced or distributed rather than massed at one point of the discourse.

16. The most impressive point in a discourse is the opening statement.

17. Artificial and mechanical devices of emphasis often defeat their purpose; the device is remembered but the proposition forgotten.

18. In spite of tradition, there is some evidence that the anticlimax order of presentation produces a more permanent, though perhaps a less moving an impression than the climax order.

19. The first argument presented has, by virtue of that priority, a distinct advantage over points of view presented later.

20. A typical educated audience, presented with subject matter in which there is already some interest, may be expected to forget about two thirds of it within one week.

21. A brief attempt by the listener to review or report the subject matter of a lecture at its close notably improves the memory of its subject matter.

22. Any device that succeeds in provoking active expression of or action upon what has been observed is a useful aid in promoting permanent impression.

CHAPTER VIII

THE PSYCHOLOGY OF PERSUASION

THE PROCESS OF CONVICTION

As in the case of advertising appeals, we may distinguish several main methods of persuasion. Chief of these are the "short-circuit," the "long-circuit," and the "rationalization" appeals. The short-circuit appeal is directed to the common human instincts and emotions, possessed by all the members of the audience. Ideas are presented which possess strong feeling tone and strike a reverberating emotional chord in the mind and experience of each hearer. Appeal is made to the moving instincts of pride, pity, self-defense, affection, banter, and rage. Through profusion of images, instances, allusions, analogies, attitudes, and the free use of the expressive reactions of voice and manner; through the appropriate sequence of topics, the adequate choice of words, and the discerning arrangement of setting and circumstance; through reliance on direct and indirect suggestion and the avoidance of the argumentative and reflective approach; and with the aid of such devices of fluency and eloquence as the speaker can summon, the crowd is led to conviction and to determination.

Some writers insist that this is always the method of the great orator. Thus Scott [60] writes:

"The orator who has welded his audience into a homogeneous crowd should never be guilty of attempting to reason with them, for by the very process of forming them into a crowd, he has deprived them of the power of critical thinking. He should affirm reasonable things and affirm conclusions which he has come to by processes of reasoning, but he should not presume to conduct the crowd through such a process. . . . No orator can sway the individuals of a crowd who does not succeed in stirring their emotions; hence successful leaders of crowds are persons of highly emotional natures, who surpass others in moving the feelings of their hearers."

THE EMOTIONAL APPEAL

There can be no doubt that the emotional appeal is characteristic of that form of public speaking classically known as oratory. But it is also true that the instincts do not always lead men aright, and that the emotions are by no means infallible guides to truth. The assumption often made is that the speaker shall have arrived at his conclusions through the use of his intelligence, but that the assent of the audience to these conclusions shall be based on their primitive instinctive and emotional reactions. As Scott says, "the mental processes of the crowd are similar to those of primitive man and hence the most effective appeal must be made to the mind of the crowd as it actually is, and not as we might assume it to be, from knowing the individuals composing it."

But the most frequent occasions of public speaking in our own time do not present audiences that are "crowds" in the psychological sense. The emotional appeal is amply played upon by the drama, the opera, the concert, the novel, poetry, the motion picture. In evangelical religious meetings, in partisan politics, in those forms of propaganda which seek to lead people to action against the verdicts of their calmer judgment, the short-circuit devices will continue to be relied upon. But the appeal to the "primitive" inevitably means control by the primitive. The course of contemporary development and the large scope of modern organization, on the other hand, constantly involve the replacement of primitive modes of reaction by motives based on understanding, insight, and intelligence. The lecturer on economics, history, finance, management, and public policy is called upon not merely to stampede his audience toward his own reasoned conclusions, but actually to increase the understanding and comprehension of his hearers. The advocate who swings the jury's verdict by impassioned utterance rather than by objective evidence and inevitable deduction prostitutes his function and jeopardizes the instruments of justice and equity. That thought and reflection are not primitive is surely no adequate excuse for betraying them.

Never before in history were audiences so intelligent and well informed, so competent and willing to follow a logical discourse. It would of course be an exaggeration to insist that social stability depends on the more universal reliance on "long-circuit," reflective, or rational technique on the part of public speakers. But it cannot be denied that modern audiences are sophisticated beyond precedence and are inclined to resent the implications of the pure emotional appeal. If it was ever necessary, for effective public speaking, to change the audience into a crowd before attempting to influence it, that necessity should rapidly disappear. The task of the average public speaker is in most cases, instead, that of converting the crowd into an audience.

The transition from social organization and public policies based on primitive loyalties and elementary passions to institutions based on intelligent co-operation and dispassionate insight resembles the transition from the family to the state. One may obey his parent or educate his child from motives of primitive and personal affection. But such elementary sentiments do not dictate one's respect for the magistrate nor the reform of public instruction. But in such a transition period, whether in the life of individuals or in the career of groups and states, much use is made of a mental process commonly known as rationalization. The rationalization appeal is an effective instrument in the hands of the public speaker, or of anyone who sets out to win an audience.

THE ART OF RATIONALIZATION

One of the striking tendencies of human beings is to act, judge, believe, or vote on strictly instinctive or emotional grounds, and then, after the act is committed or the choice made, to justify or defend it by intellectual or logical reasons. Thus, we believe in immortality because we prefer it, want it, have a deep-seated and emotional yearning for it. Having formulated our belief on these purely non-rational grounds, on the basis of a wish, we search for arguments which we can give to our neighbors in justification of it. We would, it seems, prefer them to think that we ourselves believe on the grounds of the logical arguments. Social education, indeed, has taught us that there is something childish about an attitude that lacks cogent support. But in our heart of hearts we know that first we believed, and only when our faith was challenged did we search for logical foundations.

Men buy automobiles in the same way. I buy my car because my neighbor has one, because it is the fashion to have one, because its possession will gratify my vanity or satisfy my pride. Then, having bought the car, I look about for logical justifications which I can give for my conduct. It is at this point that I discover that "It saves time," "It entertains the family," "It promotes our health," "It gives us needed relaxation," "It saves car fare," etc.

The advertising man is beginning to understand this human tendency, and advertisements will frequently be found which begin with a distinctly emotional, short-circuit appeal, thus persuading and seducing the reader. Then, at a later point, the copy writer hastens to add a series of logical reasons, which probably exercise but little influence on the prospect's own decisions. But they fortify him against the objections of his mother-in-law, his banker, or his conscience. This distinct type of appeal, which is more and more coming into prominence and clear recognition by human engineers, takes advantage in a clever and sagacious way of the "rationalizing" tendency of all of us. It is especially well calculated as a form of personal appeal in cases in which the contemplated act or conclusion would lead the individual against the expectation of his immediate social group or party or against the traditions of his early education.

In winning an audience, this technique of rationalization is to be carefully distinguished from an unguided mixture and confusion of argument and eloquence. It involves not merely the combination of rational and emotional motives, but implies their organization in a deliberate pattern in which the very motives that are emotionally aroused are given explicit foundation through inductive inferences or deductive conclusion. It assumes throughout that, just as faith without works is vain, so also passion without knowledge is treacherous.

From the point of view of social welfare, the rationalization appeal is easily capable of abuse, just as is the purely emotional appeal. But it has also its ethically and socially justifiable occasions. These are under circumstances in which the emotional appeal is required in order to arouse initial interest and adequate appreciation of the importance of the topic. Rationalized support of emotionally established convictions may thus lead to concern and action which could not have been aroused without the initial emotional stimulus. Such sinister features as the rationalization appeal presents arise not from the nature of the mental mechanisms involved, but rather from the uses to which the technique may be put. If the rationalization appeal bears an element of shadiness in its character, this is only because the instruments of darkness are ever on the alert for effective technique, and prompt in its use.

DESIRE AND CONVICTION

It is reported that Jane Addams once remonstrated with a poor woman whose customary diet was at fault, seeking to recommend to her the use of more wholesome foods. To this advice the woman of the tenements replied that she "didn't want to eat what she'd ought but what she'd ruther." That mankind believes what it wishes to believe is an old maxim, reflected and more or less philosophically justified in the pragmatic essay of William James on "The Will to Believe." This is, in a sense, just what is implied in the technique of rationalization,—that the acceptance of a proposition is determined not alone by the evidence in its favor, but first of all by the desirability of its truth. In order to secure empirical demonstration and measurement of this tendency, Lund [42] performed a series of experiments which set the facts in a dramatic light. The results are particularly striking, inasmuch as they were secured from individuals with more than high-school education, most of them from college students, who are far from being the least sophisticated members of our population.

To these individuals, several hundred in number, a list of propositions was given. Each proposition was to be rated on a scale of "belief strength," a diagram of which was also provided. On other occasions the same propositions were rated, instead, on a scale of "desirability." Proper experimental conditions were observed, so that the one rating should not be contaminated by the memory of the other. With these data, the general belief status of a given proposition can be determined and compared with its desirability. This may be done for each individual separately, or for the whole group by taking average instead of individual ratings.

The average results for a typical group are shown in the graph, page 116. Here the propositions are arranged in the order of their belief strength, beginning with the most believed and progressing down to the least believed or most disbelieved. The positions of these propositions on the *belief* scale are shown by the solid black line, which shows that the propositions chosen covered a large section of the range from total belief to total disbelief.

The dotted or broken line shows for each proposition the place assigned it on the *desire* scale. The agreement of belief with desire is remarkable. The two lines of the graph take the same general course, and the deviations of belief from desire are both infrequent and slight. In fact the coincidence of the lines is probably almost as close as would be separate determinations for either belief or desire. The correlation in rank between the order for belief and that for desire is over $+ .80$. These results, moreover, are confirmed by further experiments, using entirely different sets of propositions, chosen by other authors for other purposes, and also on different groups of people.

Here, then, we have not only a demonstration, but a

quantitative determination as well, of the mutual relations of belief and desire.   Either one of these tends to
determine the other, or else both are determined together

LUND'S CURVES, SHOWING THE CORRESPONDENCE BETWEEN STRENGTH OF
BELIEF AND DEGREE OF DESIRABILITY.

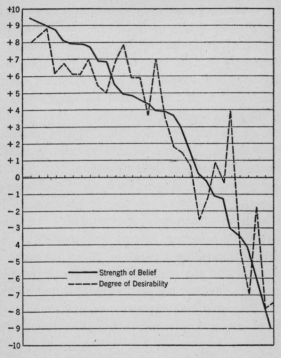

Strength of Belief
Degree of Desirability

*The strength of belief and the degree of desirability are indicated by
the position accorded each proposition on a ten point scale.   The base
line or zero point of the scale is the neutral or indifference point.   Each
vertical line thus shows the belief and the desirability of a given proposition, of which there were thirty.*

by some third factor.   No such third factor suggests
itself.   Nor is it probable that belief is the determining
factor, upon which we base our desires.   The most reasonable interpretation is that our beliefs are not de-

pendent upon the available evidence alone, but are definitely warped, even against the evidence, by our desires. In fact, more than half of the determination of our belief in a proposition seems to flow from our desires with respect to its correctness.

The conviction of an audience, therefore, is a more complex task than that of presenting sensory data and evidence for the truth of a conclusion. Since the acceptance of a conclusion, at least in the absence of explicit evidence *pro* and *con,* is contingent upon its compatibility with our desires, it is incredible that our desires should become entirely inert with the appearance of the sensory data. There can be no doubt that, even in the presence of factual evidence, our desires constitute a dynamic influence, leading us to overlook, to emphasize, to select, to interpret, in their direction.

In persuading an audience, then, one fundamental procedure is that of linking up the proposition to be advanced with an atmosphere of desirability, or attaching to its antithesis a feeling tone of undesirability. That is to say, the proposition should be given its place in the scale of values, in the wish and strife life of the auditors. And since this preliminary attitude will in part determine the evaluation and interpretation of evidence, it should, to be most effective, precede rather than follow the sensory evidence.

This process should not be confused with the sheer appeal to prejudice and the arousal of violent emotion which cannot be sustained. For among the desires of human beings are those to know the truth, to be rationally guided, to avoid being duped by our animal urges, to escape gullibility, to evade chicanery, to recognize the charlatan and demagogue, to respect ourselves. Indeed these desires, though perhaps less violent upon outbreak, nevertheless persist and succeed over the more episodic desires of revenge, jealousy, rivalry, and excitement. The discriminating performer must thus decide whether he is seeking for momentary action or for permanent attitude on the part of his auditors, for his own technique should vary with his desire.

THE VARIETIES OF EVIDENCE

The statement that modern audiences are sophisticated and reasonable beyond precedence should not be misconstrued into an exaggeration of the average human intelligence. Willingness to think is not to be confused with ability to think soundly or profoundly. The modern audience may be willing to listen to what it is pleased to call evidence, but its idea of the nature of evidence is far from that of the logician or of the scientific man. Vigorous assertion, a figure of speech, a cleverly suggested inference, personal innuendo, a witty retort, the quotation of irrelevant but esteemed authority, the display of erudition, easily lead awry the thinking of the average man. This influence is quite aside from the appeal to his emotion.

It is not quite true that the average man reasons scarcely at all. On the contrary, he has a passion for argument, and prides himself in it; but he reasons stupidly. He mistakes coincidence for proof, correlation for causality, confidence for necessity, publicity for expertness, and appearance for reality. Habit, suggestion, and imitation constitute his instruments of thinking, as distinguished from his emotional reactions, and his inadequate background of knowledge, coupled with the urgency of his needs, makes him the ready prey of the fakir and the charlatan.

Scientific evidence consists of facts and data that may

be independently interpreted and put to the test of controlled observation. There is another type of evidence,
as it is called, which is more familiar to the average man,
and which has taken its place as the most conspicuous
type of evidence in court procedure. It takes the form
of vigorous, positive, and sworn assertion by some individual that such and such things are true. Expert testi-
mony is especially likely to take this form, because judge
and jury are not competent to understand nor interpret
the original observations.

An expert was once called upon in court to prove the
truth of certain statements as to the validity of the methods he had used. For several hours he presented data
and facts which to his mind proved the statements and
the methods to be valid. But this array of actual evidence was rejected as not constituting proof. Finally he
took his cue from a more practiced witness who took the
stand during his rest period. When next examined he
stated simply that to his own knowledge and from his
own observation the statements were true. This confident assertion was at once accepted as adequate proof,
and the case proceeded without further delay. It is this
type of oracular evidence, the dogmatic assertion of a
respectable person, a book, or a newspaper, upon which
the conclusions of the average man are based and his acts
determined.

The myth about "the hard-headed business man" dies
even more slowly than do the stories of Santa Claus, the
rainbow, and the stork. Only when, as in the case of
manufacturing costs, overhead, and transportation
charges, the facts stick into him like thorns in the flesh,
will the average man of business worry over facts. Suggestibility and mysticism find in him their last strong-
hold. For the most part, he is content with tradition,

opinion, authority, the sanction of prestige, and other forms of bluff. In consultation work, five men ask for unsupported opinion for every two who are interested in the data on which that opinion is based. Even in courts of law the question is not, "What facts can you adduce which bear on the point at issue?" but instead, "Doctor, is it your opinion that . . . ?"

The error of relying on the cheap modes of persuasion is similar to that involved in the control of children by the fear of bogies. Immediate conduct may be controlled by invoking fear of the "bad man," the "policeman," the "goblins," and "eternal incineration." But eventually the trickery of these devices will be discovered by the more astute at least. The typical result of such discovery is resentment, suspicion of all authority, obstinacy, and general skepticism. When fear of bogies is dispelled by better knowledge, faith in sounder principles of control is also undermined.

The salesman who resorts to trickery and unsound evidence may make an immediate sale. But he may by that same act destroy the confidence of an otherwise steady customer, impair the good will of his firm, and stiffen resistance against sounder inducements. Impassioned persuasion and specious argument, in other words, may determine a nomination, provoke a mutiny, inflame a momentary lust for personal revenge. But such devices also have their kick-back, and are perhaps in the end their own remedy. When the spell is broken, another may take its place, or sounder evidence may be encountered. He who cried, "Wolf, Wolf!" when no danger was near may suffer from the apathy of an oft exploited audience on occasions of genuine peril.

The reliance on specious evidence is by no means the special prerogative of the average man. The educated and more intelligent also succumb to it, and may cling to it until brute facts compel its sacrifice. A few examples of the use of the specious in high places may serve to exhibit the sort of fallacy which in humbler minds is effective at the moment but suffers from the test of experience. Such fallacies have, to be sure, been described for ages in the textbooks of logic, and there given dignified names. But the formal study of logic, for one thing, is no longer fashionable. Moreover, even those who know the technical names of logical errors are often prone to commit them.

SPECIOUS ARGUMENTS BASED ON CORRELATION

The director of a Bureau of Industrial Research(!), writing in no less imposing a place than one of our "quality group" magazines, remarks that, "Soldiers who had an institutional training in orphanages and the like were more liable to shell-shock," and concludes that, "The children of divorced parents, children brought up in institutions, children who have been overdisciplined—these are the adults who suffer a high incidence of nervous breakdown." This type of "demonstrative" or "anecdotal" argument is among the most specious of the forms of proof. As a matter of fact, measurements show that "inferior intelligence," with the general organic incompetence it involves, is in great measure responsible both for nervous breakdown and for orphan-asylum residence. The mere correlation of these latter two facts is no evidence of their causal relation, and the argument is a neat case of the confusion between correlation and causation.

The Research Bulletin(!) of a large public-school system, quoting with approval from a report by a Federal Bureau, remarks:

"Each day spent in high school is worth $25 to each pupil, each day spent in college $55.55. This is more than the average boy or girl can earn by leaving school and going to work.

"Only one in a hundred of our people is a college graduate, yet 36% of every 100 congressmen have been college graduates, while 50% of our Presidents, 54% of our Vice-Presidents, 69% of our Supreme Court Judges, and 87% of our Attorney Generals have had college degrees.

"Does education pay?   IT DOES."

This type of argument has often been used by educational propagandists, who, of all people, ought to face their audience with cogent data rather than with specious argument.   It is obvious enough that all the facts cited show is not that "education pays," but simply that high educational attainment is possible only for those who are also otherwise competent, and perhaps the further fact that the more competent people are the more likely to remain in school by choice.   Again the fallacy is that of mistaking correlation for causal relation between two facts, both of which depend upon a third feature which is not even mentioned.   And the intended implication of the argument, however correct it may be in its own right, is only absurdly based upon such treacherous reasoning. Surely, if going to college, and the like, has such efficacious virtue, we ought to lower the requirements so that larger numbers could share the mysterious benefit.   And if Phi Beta Kappa honors are so potent in increasing wages or in procuring distinction as they are said to be in these pamphlets, we ought to confer this honor on a much larger proportion of our graduates than is now the custom.   Such effective remedies should be dispensed only with generosity.

An eminent biologist, in a popular article on "Alcohol and the Duration of Life," reports that abstainers and moderate users of alcohol live some five years longer than do heavy and steady drinkers. He concludes therefore that "heavy drinking distinctly shortens life." Now this may well be the case, but it is far from shown by the data presented. Thus it might well be simply that sick people, injured people, deformed persons, and others who for reason of one or another sort of organic inferiority, see in life's activities no great boon, more readily seek to "drown their sorrow" in "heavy and steady drinking." If this were the case, and alcohol entirely innocuous, heavy drinkers would have shorter lives (because of their organic inferiorities and native weakness). Once more the fallacy is that of confusing correlation with causal sequence. And however profound the truth of the conclusion, the specious nature of the evidence is not only in itself lamentable, but is also calculated to foster shallow public thinking.

"POST HOC ERGO PROPTER HOC"

Post hoc ergo propter hoc is the designation long ago given by logicians to a type of fallacious thinking that is often played upon by the public speaker. Moreover, this type of argument is so often accepted by the average man that it neatly illustrates the assertion that the typical human mind does seek to reason but is unable to avoid reasoning of a low order. It ought to be sufficiently obvious that the mere fact that B follows A is not adequate evidence that A is the cause of B. Yet just this assumption is what constitutes the "post hoc" fallacy.

Thus a recent President of the National Education Association is quoted as using the following argument before a large and supposedly intelligent audience.

"In the last six years I have crossed the continent six times and in one year I have been in 25 states. I believe that I am in a position to draw conclusions as to the good working of the prohibition amendment, and I assert that there are more children in the schools now than there ever were before the dry law and that these children are better clothed and have better filled lunch baskets than ever before."

Our point is of course not that the conclusion is untrue, but merely that the evidence is insufficient. Many things (such as the Japanese earthquake) followed the dry law enactment; but mere subsequent occurrence does not constitute one thing the effect of another. And many things preceded the increase in school attendance and the "better filled lunch baskets" (the invention of flying machines, for example); but mere antecedent occurrence does not constitute one thing the cause of another.

AFFIRMING THE CONSEQUENT

One of the most common fallacies utilized by the public speaker and propagandist is the familiar one of "affirming the consequent." Thus most of the theories of the occult, of popular character analysis, the doctrines of psychic healing, psycho-analytic explanations of dreams, of neuroses, of cures, and the like, have been made to carry conviction by this technique. The argument runs in the following way.

> If A-B-C is true, then we will find X-Y-Z.
> Upon investigation, we find X-Y-Z.
> Therefore A-B-C is true.

Or more concretely, as follows: "If suppressed unconscious complexes are responsible for hysteric symptoms, it follows that a careful exploration of infantile experience and discovery of juvenile psychic injuries will relieve the symptoms. Now we find that this method of therapy works in actual practice. Therefore[!] hysteria is due to unconscious complexes." But this type of argument is actually only that of the insane delusion, which might run in something like the following way: "If the devil has put poison into my coffee, I will have a pain in my stomach. Now I have a pain in my stomach. Therefore[!] the devil has put poison in my coffee."

IMPRESSIVENESS OF WORDS

As a last illustration, we may cite the type of conviction that comes from the credence of mere assertion and the impressiveness of dignified or technical words. Thus a razor company announced in its advertising, "a new triumph of American inventive genius of startling interest to every man with a beard to shave . . . for the first time in any razor micrometric control of the blade position" made possible by "the fulcrum shoulder, overhanging cap, and channeled guard." A diagram showed "how the blade is biflexed between overhanging cap and fulcrum shoulder. It is flexed once into the inside curve of the cap. This is the minor flexure—the curve for easy gliding action and play of the wrist in shaving. It is flexed a second time—more sharply and in a shorter radius—by the grip of the overhanging cap the whole length of the fulcrum shoulder."

Poffenberger [54] gave copies of these advertisements, well illustrated, to fifty-seven men students, together with a series of seven questions intended to test both their belief in the new razor and their understanding of it. He reports the results in the following words.

"The answers to these questions showed that all the students agreed that the new razor was better than the old one, and that they would rather pay $5 for the new one than $1 or $2 for the old one. In supporting their belief they were allowed to consult the advertisement as much as they wished. They quoted the 'fulcrum shoulder,' which made possible 'micrometric control of the blade position,' but not one of them could explain how the micrometric control was obtained or what advantage there would be in having such a micrometric control. They believed that the 'channeled guard' was an improvement although they could not tell why it was an improvement. As to the importance of major and minor flexures they were entirely ignorant."

It is unnecessary for our purpose to indicate more of the various fallacies that readily creep into ordinary reasoning. These examples are here given only to illustrate the general statement already made, that what is often called "appeal to the emotions" is in many cases instead simply specious argument and shallow reasoning. It is important, in understanding the reaction of any group, to bear in mind the distinction between cogent and valid argument, in the first place; specious and fallacious evidence, in the second place; and emotional appeal, in the third place. It is important because for the average man the second type of persuasion is likely to be effective as in the first or the third, and failure to keep these distinctions in mind readily leads to fanciful and mythical ideas about the modes of shaping public opinion.

THE MIND OF THE AVERAGE MAN

He who would win an audience should have the clearest possible notion of the general level of understanding and sagacity of his auditors. The term "average audience" has of course two very different meanings. It may mean the average audience of the type the particular speaker usually confronts,—the average audience of teachers, the average audience of labor delegates, the average audience of college students, of music lovers, of motion-picture habitués, etc. As to the characteristics of such audiences. little definite contribution can be made by the psychologist, beyond tentative indications of the average intelligence of these groups.

In another and perhaps more common sense the "average audience" means an audience of average people. This is an audience in which the various degrees of understanding and sagacity found in the population at large are proportionately represented, and in which the predominant number of auditors are "average people." Ideas of what the mind of the "average man" is like were extremely vague until recent large-scale intelligence measurements were undertaken. Thanks to these investigations, it is now possible to describe in fairly definite terms the mind of the average man, and such a description should be in the mental background of every speaker who attempts to win an "average audience" in this sense of the term. What can we say about the mental characteristics and capacity of the average man? The average adult is still "at large," but data from the examination of the draft army in the World War are available,[75] and we know also the characteristic abilities of children whose mental age is equal to that of the average adult as shown by the army data. The following section gives at least the best information we have on the subject.

The tabulation gives in brief a few things that statistical records reveal concerning the average records of the American male population, and the mental characteristics of individuals with average adult mental age.

Height	about 67 inches
Weight	about 150 pounds
Brain weight	about 1300 grams, 2% of body weight
Pulse rate	about 70 per minute
Daily sleep	about 9 hours
Age at death	about 53
Age of marriage	early

Number of children	about 3 or 4
Salary or wages	about $1,200
Education	sixth grade
Vocabulary	about 7,500 words
Some words he can explain	nerve, insure, juggler, shrewd
Words he cannot explain	Mars, coinage, charter, philanthropy
Some distinctions he can make	three differences between a president and a king
Distinctions he cannot explain	difference between poverty and misery; difference between evolution and revolution
Problems he can solve in 1 minute	how many pencils for 50 cents if 2 cost 5 cents cost of 7 feet of cloth at 15 cents a yard
A problem he fails on	in a large box are 4 smaller ones, in each of which are four still smaller. How many in all?
Memory span	7 digits 17 word sentence
Some things he can understand	meaning of words—revenge, pity, envy, charity, justice
Some things he cannot understand	difference between character and reputation difference between laziness and idleness what is meant by avarice, conscientious
Average mental age	about 14 years
Intelligence Quotient	100
Occupations whose average mental level is the same as this	carpenter, plumber, cook, blacksmith
Occupations whose average mental level is lower than this	tailor, barber, farmer, horse shoer, boilermaker
Occupations whose average mental level is higher than this	bookkeeper, filing clerk, band musician, dentist, stenographer, accountant, physician

THE AVERAGE MAN'S BELIEFS

It would be instructive to have an inventory of the beliefs held and the convictions cherished by the average man. No data of this kind are available, although on levels representing greater intelligence and more information surprising results have been found. Suppose for example that the following propositions were presented to the average man. How many of them would he accept as true?

That all men are born equal and only lack of opportunity keeps some from becoming famous or rich.

That all Mormons believe in and practice polygamy, having at least three and sometimes seven wives.

That all French women are beautiful, and all actresses immoral.

That people are more dishonest and children more impudent than they were when he was a boy.

That a doctor can tell from the bumps on your head whether you have a sense of humor.

That nasty medicine is more powerful than that with a pleasant taste or odor.

That feebleminded children will develop more rapidly than others at the age of puberty.

That dreams are prophetic and one skilled in the art (as a gypsy) can tell from them what is going to happen to you.

Some of the words in these propositions would not be understood by the man of average intelligence, but the chances are that this would not deter him from accepting all the propositions as sound.

Since no careful inventory of the beliefs of the average man has been made, these suggestions are purely tentative. But studies have on several occasions been made of the beliefs accepted by various superior groups of individuals, with astonishing results. Thus Nixon [52] presented to classes of college students beginning their study of psychology a list of thirty statements. These were each to be marked true or false according to the opinion of the individual student. There were 140 women and 219 men in the groups so investigated. The following table gives some of the statements, with the number of men and the number of women who accepted each proposition as true.

STATEMENT	PER CENT OF COLLEGE STUDENTS WHO MARKED IT AS TRUE	
	Men	Women
1. The number of man's senses is five . .	76%	78%
2. Adults sometimes become feebleminded from over study	56	57
3. Long, slender hands indicate an artistic nature	42	52
4. A man's character can be read by noting the size and location of special developments of the head	40	51
5. An expectant mother, by fixing her mind on a subject, can influence the character of her unborn child	38	44
6. Many eminent men have been feebleminded as children	36	25
7. Any physical or mental disease can be contracted by thinking about it . .	31	44
8. All men are created equal in capacity for achievement	23	20
9. People born under the influence of certain planets show the influence in their characters	15	20
10. Certain lines in a person's hand foretell his future	8	25

Trotter [65] has offered suggestions concerning the make-up of the average mind, as follows:

"If we examine the mental furniture of the average man we shall find it made up of a vast number of judgments of a very precise kind, upon subjects of very great variety, complexity and difficulty. He will have fairly settled views upon the origin and nature of the universe, and upon what he will probably call its meaning; he will have conclusions as to what is to happen to him at death and after, as to what is and what should be the basis of conduct.

"He will know how the country should be governed, and why it is going to the dogs; why this piece of legislation is good and that bad. He will have strong views upon military and naval strategy, the principles of taxation, the use of alcohol, vaccination, the treatment of influenza, the prevention of hydrophobia, the teaching of Greek, upon what is permissible in art, satisfactory in literature and hopeful in science."

The interesting thing about this evaluation of the mind of the average man is its gross exaggeration of the creature. The picture here drawn is more like a description of the average high-school or college graduate, who is as a matter of fact very exceptional.

The popular opinion of what an average citizen is like requires substantial correction. Even professional publicists and popular leaders, presumably in close touch with humanity, often express fantastic notions on this subject. Thus a distinguished British journalist, in an article entitled "An Average Englishman Speaks," begins as follows:

"Let us take as our average Englishman the fairly intelligent, moderately well-educated, middle-aged business man. He . . . goes for a foreign trip now and then. . . . Occasionally he thinks about . . . his game of golf, which keeps him fit."

An American publicist, referring to the personnel of the League of Nations, labors under the strange delusion that the representatives on it are "average men." He writes:

"It is not a body of super-men. The delegates are ordinary human beings. . . . When a nation sends delegates to the League they are more or less a cross section of its average intelligence. So the League of Nations is the average of the intelligence of the nations that compose it."

Finally, a metropolitan newspaper, in describing the members of a certain jury, refers to them as typifying "the average American citizen." The jury consisted of the following:

> An architect's clerk.
> Wife of a national bank cashier.
> Retired druggist and manufacturer.
> Western agent for New York manufacturer.
> Owner of a city dry-goods store.
> A certified public accountant.
> Wife of a plumbing contractor.
> Wife of an oil salesman.
> A widow.
> A hardware clerk.
> A retired restaurant employee.
> An independent farmer who once owned a store.

It seems wholly likely that this list of jurors represents at least the upper 25 per cent, rather than the average of the population, and that so far as intelligence is concerned, every one of them was superior to the average man or woman.

Such a picture as that drawn by Trotter is however fairly applicable to the average of those persons who are likely to be found in audiences by most speakers. This is to say that a typical audience is not drawn from the average of the population, nor does it represent fairly a cross section of the population.

It is the average man as we have described him instead, who represents the average parent, met as an individual; the average dictator of the fortunes and destinies of a family; the average voter at elections. It is his privilege, if he has enough influential friends or supporters, to become a member of the school board, the mayor of a city, a judge, or a senator. It is his characteristics, and those of his average wife, which, under the laws of heredity, will largely determine the mental caliber of coming generations. This result will be modified only in so far as the level is pulled still lower by those inferior to him, who tend on the whole to have still larger families than he does, whereas those above him tend constantly toward limitation of offspring.

THE AVERAGE AUDIENCE

Of course not all the members of the "average audience," in the sense in which we have been using this term, will conform to the description we have just given, although this type will predominate. It will represent approximately 50 per cent of the audience, one fourth of the group being lower than even this picture would suggest, the other fourth being superior to it.

An approximate and concrete picture of the composition of such a group may be secured by combining the army data on occupations and that on the frequency of various mental ratings in the draft army, adding other data now available on groups not included in this source. Instead of representing degree of intelligence by scores or quotients, we may choose for each section of the group such well-known occupations as have been found to rate at that point or thereabouts in average mental competence.

The chart on page 134 does not pretend to tell an exact story, although the data on which it is based are of strictly scientific nature and have been recorded in the literature of mental measurement. The chart gives only the averages of groups, and does not, for example, imply that all

Defectives Incompetents Dependents Mental age under 10 years	Laborers Cobblers Tailors Miners **Teamsters** Grade-school pupils Mental age about 12 years	Plumbers Conductors Carpenters Brakemen Mechanics Chauffeurs Policemen Telephone operators Poor high-school students Finished the grade school Mental age about 14 years THE AVERAGE MAN	Nurses Accountants Bookkeepers Stenographers Dentists Filing clerks College students Mental age about 16 years	Professions Executives Univ. graduates Superior adult level
5%	20%	50%	20%	5%

policemen are mentally fourteen years old and have finished the grade schools. The individuals in any of the occupational groups diverge widely from their average, and there is much overlapping of the groups. The speaker will, however, have formed a fairly definite impression of the average mental level of the individuals of these groups from his contact with them. The chart will help to indicate their relative frequency in the audience taken at random from the population at large, if mental level, rather than actual occupational activity is considered.

EXPERIMENTAL STUDIES OF AUDIENCE REACTIONS

Experimental study of the way in which an audience reacts to a speaker's arguments is still in the preliminary stage. We have already reviewed some of the investigations dealing with such topics as attention, interest, and memory. There have been also attempts to register the shifts of opinion and conviction produced by listening to debates and argument. It has also been suggested that recently devised scales for measuring personal and individual "attitude" toward topics might be used in determining the initial and final state of opinion in the audience and thus measuring the effect of material presented to it in the form of discussion or argument.

A series of analyses of audience ballots reported by Woodward [71] will serve to indicate some of the possibilities of studying audience reactions. Over a period of three years student debaters appeared before 118 audiences, debating eight different questions. Ballots were distributed, on which the members of each audience voted, expressing, before the debate, their attitude as affirmative, negative, or neutral. After the debate they voted again, indicating any change of opinion, or any strengthening or weakening of opinion. In all, 43.3 per cent of the members of the various audiences submitted these double ballots, and the shifts in opinion were put to use in deciding the debate contests. Although the results might have been materially changed had all the auditors voted, the results secured on the smaller number at least suggest the possibilities of such analyses, and the nature of the information that might be derived from them.

Among the results suggested, the following are typical and of some special interest. Change of opinion is more likely to occur in those initially undecided; that is, neutral votes are more likely to change into definite opinions, than definite opinions are to change. Only 16 per cent of the neutral votes remained unchanged after the debates, whereas 30 per cent of the affirmative and the same per cent of the negative opinions remained unchanged. Neutral opinions appear thus to be less stable than initial opinions for or against. Affirmative and negative opinions appear about equally capable of change.

These results vary considerably with the topic. In fact, on three of the questions here studied, between 50 and 60 per cent of the initial affirmative or negative opinions remained unchanged as the result of hearing the debate. The investigator suggests that these were questions on which the audiences were least well informed. If it is true that on questions on which the listener is relatively more ignorant, argument has less effect in producing a shift of opinion, this is an important fact for the public speaker to know. Perhaps it is on just such topics that wishes, rather than data, are the determinants of opinion.

On most subjects, when neutrals shifted unequally toward the two possible sides, this shift was greater toward the side that already had the greater number of votes. Apparently even the undecided incline somewhat more strongly toward one than toward another side, or are more easily shifted in one direction than another, and the social vote is a useful indication of this direction.

Considering all the questions and all the audiences, however, neutrals are as likely to shift in one direction as in the other, 41 per cent shifting toward the affirmative and 43 per cent toward the negative side of these questions after the debates.

In the case of those who initially had definite opinions, it is of great interest to observe that the effect of debate is three times as likely to strengthen these opinions as it is to weaken them. Thus 52 per cent of those whose opinions were initially affirmative reported their opinions to have been strengthened by the debate. In the case of those whose opinions were negative instead, the same figure resulted. On the other hand only 17 per cent of those who had definite opinions, whether affirmative or negative, reported these opinions weakened. The net effect of listening to debate appears therefore to be to strengthen opinions already held, and to shift the undecided toward those opinions that are already held by the majority. It is easier, apparently, to shift a neutral to a definite opinion than it is to change or to weaken an opinion already formed.

PRACTICAL CONCLUSIONS

1. The members of an audience are more alike in their instincts and emotions than in capacity to follow logical reasoning; hence emotional appeals or topics will more uniformly and generally influence them.

2. Modern audiences are more homogeneously selected than formerly and their increasing sophistication gives added value

to the appearance of logical persuasion, even if the true basis of the appeal is emotional and even if the logic is fallacious.

3. When a suggested act or conclusion would lead the individual against social pressure or group sanctions, there is a special effectiveness in the "rationalization" appeal, in which an attitude or conclusion, first aroused emotionally, is given subsequent logical justification and support.

4. The beliefs of an audience do not depend on evidence alone; they are definitely warped, even against the evidence, by desires and hopes.

5. To smooth the way for logical acceptance of an idea, first align the idea with the desires and wishes of the audience, reserving its logical proof for a later step.

6. The average man prides himself on his rationality, but his conception of evidence and of the nature of proof is naïve and easily satisfied, even by specious and invalid argument.

7. Susceptibility to cheap and fallacious modes of persuasion is by no means limited to the average man; even the "hardheaded business man" is seldom an exception to the rule.

8. Many supposedly emotional appeals are not emotional, but only the unrestrained use of metaphor, analogy, and the loose resort to fallacious argument, which succeeds only because it assumes logical form.

9. The fear of bogies is a dangerous instrument; when it is dispelled by better knowledge, faith in sounder principles of control is also undermined.

10. Prevalent forms of specious argument to which the gullible easily yield are (*a*) confusing anecdote with proof; (*b*) mistaking analogy for evidence; (*c*) mistaking correlation with causal relation; (*d*) the *argumentum ad hominem;* (*e*) affirming the consequent; and (*f*) confusing obscurity for profundity.

11. Even those who know the names of logical fallacies often succumb to them and are guilty of their use.

12. The average man, as characterized by what is now known about his mental equipment and beliefs, merits the astonished study of every public performer.

13. Opinion appears to be more easily formed in the undecided than it is to be changed in those who have already adopted a point of view.   Neutral opinions are less stable than committed ones.

14. Change of opinion, through hearing argument, appears to be more likely to occur in connection with topics on which the audience is already better informed.

15. The net effect of listening to argument appears to be strengthening of opinions already held and shift of neutral opinion in the direction already indicated by the majority.

CHAPTER IX

DIRECTING ACTION

DEFINING THE ACT

The principles involved in directing the action of the audience will vary considerably, no doubt, with the type of audience, the occasion for action, and the actual authority of the speaker. There is little that can be enumerated here beyond the simple rules of suggestion which apply to all human relations. Whether the action is to take place at once, as in the case of a deliberative assembly called on to vote on an issue, or whether the action is deferred until a time subsequent to the dispersal of the audience, as in the case of a political campaign, one principle should never be forgotten. This is the principle of suggesting in specific and definite terms the nature, place, and method of the desired response.

The treasurer of a society was frequently observed to rise at periodic intervals during the year and, pointing out the urgent need for funds, in the form of regular membership dues, to request that members kindly pay their assessments. No specifications were given beyond this gentle and vague suggestion, and as a consequence few assessments were paid, in spite of the frequent requests. The treasurer should have closed the first request by indicating at which door she would stand at the close of the meeting, or by writing her name and address on the board, or by some other such specific device should have suggested definite action at definite time or place.

Such an illustration is to be sure a far cry from the field of oratory, but it represents one of the real cases in which an audience must be effectively handled if it is to be won.

It is in just this spirit that the salesman always has his order book ready and requests the converted prospect immediately to "sign on the dotted line." The advertiser places a coupon in the corner of the page, or is sure to give his firm name, address, or place of business. Revival meetings which succeed provide specific altar directions —"Married men gather at the right of the platform," "All the dentists in the congregation now sing the third verse," "March up the aisle while the choir sings Onward Christian Soldiers." The climax of this specification of response is seen in the most completely polarized audience that we have described, that of the organized team or regiment or orchestra.

THE LAWS OF SUGGESTION

In much the same way, the remaining general laws of suggestion, which have been frequently formulated and illustrated, apply as fully to the winning of an audience to action as they do to the handling of individuals. We need here do no more than suggest these by a brief statement indicating the nature of each of the principles.

1. The strength of a suggestion depends in part of the degree to which it seems to be of spontaneous origin, an act of the individual's own initiative. Arrogance and domination are at once and instinctively resented and resisted. The more indirect the suggestion, the more it can be made to be an original determination or plan or conclusion on the part of the listener, the greater its dynamic power.

2. Within the limits of the law just indicated, the

dynamic power of a suggestion will be the greater, the more forcefully and vividly it is presented. This is especially true when the suggested act is in harmony with the pre-established habits and tendencies. When the suggestion violates life-long habits and instincts, attempts to be forceful and vigorous usually lapse into arrogance and thereby defeat their own purpose.

3. It is more effective to suggest the desired response directly than it is to argue against a response that is not desired. Suggestion is most active at its positive pole, and the negative suggestion tends to defeat its own purpose. The Old Covenant with its "Thou Shalt Not" was readily displaced by the New Covenant with its simple, positive "Thou Shalt."

4. The action power of a suggestion varies directly with the prestige of its source. The more we revere a speaker, for any reason whatsoever, the greater confidence we tend to place in anything he may say, and the more prone we are to imitate him and to adopt his suggestions, even when they are unsupported by sufficient reason.

5. The strength of a suggestion will be determined in part by the degree of internal resistance it encounters. That suggestion will be most effective which can call to its aid or appropriate the dynamic force of some other impulse that is already active or latent. Suggestions to violate life-long habits, firmly fixed moral feelings, and sacred relationships are impotent, even during the pronounced suggestibility of the hypnotic trance.

6. The strength of a suggestion varies with the frequency with which it is met. But mere mechanical repetition avails little unless the repeated suggestion is attended to with interest. Experiment shows that repetition of advertising appeals is twice as effective when the

form, style, and expression is varied, with constant
theme, as when exact duplication of previous appeals is
used. Repetition accompanied by sufficient variety to
lend interest but with sufficient uniformity to acquire a
constant meaning, produces a genuine cumulative effect.

7. In appealing over the short circuit for a specific
line of action, no interference, substitute, rival idea, or
opposing action should be suggested. Such an idea
merely impedes the action power of the first suggestion,
by inviting comparison and thus involves deliberate
choice and hesitation.

There is an apparent contradiction between what we
have just said concerning the advantages of repetition
with variety and LeBon's [40] assertion that "Affirmation
has no real influence unless it be constantly repeated,
and so far as possible *in the same terms.*" Both principles, however, are valid. The apparent contradiction
arises from the fact that a suggestion or affirmation may
have two very distinct functions.

PSYCHOLOGY OF THE SLOGAN

For the purposes of maintaining attention and interest, of linking up the impression with the individual's
background of experience, and of persuading him toward
a general course of action, repetition with variation
seems to be the most effective measure. But another
function of the suggestion, and an important one, as we
have seen, is that of specifying and giving precise defini-
tion to the act. Here the principle of repetition in the
same terms, of duplication instead of variation, has its
advantages. This is what is involved in the psychology
of the slogan. "Swat the fly," an exhortation constantly
reiterated, defines the act, and serves effectually to perpetuate the decision beyond the immediate occasion of

its formation. It crystallizes the propaganda of a whole evening's program, remains with the auditor as a succinct formula of action. Becoming a slogan, it unites in a common decision audiences geographically remote from each other and readily spreads to individuals not present at the local program.

Along with the demand for a concrete symbol,—a seal, a flag, a color, a badge, trademark, battle cry, or other single device for representing and suggesting the essence of an abstract principle or a group enterprise,—goes the popular craving for a terse slogan which will take the place of careful description, conceal the lack of real understanding, identify, and rally the devotees of a leader or party, and serve as a convenient challenge to the enemy. Political leaders, as well as juvenile organizers and advertisers, have learned the practical utility of the slogan, and the individualism and partnership of enterprise and control give the practice respectable standing in spite of its dubious psychological implications.

HATE AND FEAR

Along with the power of the slogan should be mentioned the unifying effect of participation in a common punishment or deprivation. The levy of a tax at once establishes bonds of community between individuals who are liable to it, however dispersed they may be. Limitations and regulations imposed on the individual's personal ration of sugar, flour, or milk go far toward arousing to active belligerency a population apathetic or resistant to the progress of military operations and the plans of the chief of staff. In the fusion of heterogeneous elements of a population into an effective social group nothing is more potent than a common hatred or a common fear. Any common emotion tends to have this consolidating effect on an audience, but on the whole it is said that mobs are more easily organized for malicious than for ennobling enterprises.

Such a statement, implying the malicious predisposition of the group, is scarcely based on evidence that is either objective or controlled. In the first place, it is commonly made of the mob as distinguished from the audience, which is a differently organized group. And the statement is usually based on historical evidence which concerns, in the main, groups manifesting relatively low degrees of intelligence, and therefore relatively low degrees of inhibition of that "proneness to error" which is characteristic of the simple mind. Furthermore, the difficulty of objectively demonstrating the truth of such an assertion is shown by the subjective and variable nature of the criteria which must be employed in distinguishing the "malicious" from the "ennobling."

Perhaps what lies behind this frequent assertion is the fact that anger and fear are emotions most readily recognized in others. Experiments show not only that adults agree quite unanimously on the significance of the facial expressions of these emotions, but that children correctly interpret them at an early age. Now the signs of emotion on the part of others readily serve as cues to the excitement of these emotions in ourselves. The more definitely these expressive signs are recognized and understood, the more easily and unanimously will the exciting words of the speaker be re-enforced by the expressive reactions of neighboring auditors. It is perhaps in part for this reason that audiences are so readily moved to fear and anger.

Numerous experiments have been performed to measure the relative ease and accuracy of the interpretations of facial expressions. The investigations quite generally agree that *pleasure* is most easily and surely identified, or at least most unequivocally expressed. *Pain* comes definitely next in ease and accuracy, then *fear, hate, anger*. Such emotions as *surprise, contempt, doubt, disgust, wonder*, and *amazement* are less equivocally expressed, less unanimously identified by adults, and correctly recognized by children only in their later years.

An illustration of the type of evidence on which such conclusions are based is afforded by some of the experiments of G. S. Gates.[18, 19] This investigator, using photographs of the same face, studied the accuracy with which the facial expressions were recognized. She concludes that:

"The evidence from the testing shows, then, that the probable order of difficulty for the pictures (from least to greatest) is for children—Laughter, Pain, Anger, Fear, Surprise and Scorn. This differs from that found for adults where the order is— Laughter and Scorn, Fear, Anger, Pain and Surprise."

The approximate ages at which, in this and later studies by the same author, expressive reactions are understood correctly from photographs, by at least three fourths of the children tested, were as follows:

Amusement, laughter, glee.........by the age of three or four.
Anger, rage, pain, and suffering.....by the age of six or seven.
Fear, terror, horror..............by the age of eight.
Defiance ....by the age of ten.
Pity or sympathy, and scorn.......by the age of eleven.
Surprise, amazement ....by the age of twelve.
Wonder, admiration, and suspicion..by adults only.

The important point in the present connection is that the consolidation and integration of the audience depends not alone upon the actions of the leader, but also upon the contributory signs afforded constantly by the attitudes and expressions of each individual to his neighbor. The organization of the group for one purpose or for another, therefore, depends in part on the quickness and certainty or accuracy with which these contributory influences spread.

We might therefore expect that the most contagious emotion in an audience would be amusement. Next would come anger, pain, and fear. Amusement does not tend to lead to further action, hence does not promote overt crowd organization. But the latter emotions lead to further overt acts of protection, punishment, and revenge. It is the readiness with which these emotions spread that seems to facilitate the organization of the crowd for what are likely to be called "malicious purposes," as distinguished from the milder reactions involved in pity, wonder, surprise, or sympathy. At least the experimental results are consistent with such an interpretation.

AUDIENCES AND MOBS

It has been popular, in the literature of group psychology, to belittle the function of intelligence in the mental processes of an audience. Thus LeBon [40] insists that:

"As soon as a few individuals are gathered together they constitute a crowd, and although they should be distinguished men of learning, they assume all the characteristics of crowds with respect to the matter outside their specialty. . . . From the moment that they form part of a crowd the learned man and the ignoramus are equally incapable of observation."

Again he refers to:

"the slight importance of the mental level of the different elements composing a crowd, so far as the decisions it comes to are concerned. . . . When a deliberative assembly is called upon to give its opinion on a question not entirely technical, intelligence stands for nothing. For instance a gathering of scientific men or artists, owing to the mere fact that they form an assemblage, will not deliver judgments on general subjects sensibly different from those rendered by a gathering of masons or grocers. . . . The decisions affecting matters of general interest come to by an assembly of men of distinction, but specialists in different walks of life, are not sensibly superior to the decisions that would be adopted by a gathering of imbeciles."

This assumed "mental inferiority of all collectivities," whatever their composition, leads LeBon to emphatic advice on the way to influence assemblies to action:

"Crowds are not to be influenced by reasoning and can only comprehend rough-and-ready associations of ideas. The orators who know how to make an impression on them always appeal in consequence to their sentiments and never to their reason. . . . An orator wishing to move a crowd must make an abusive use of violent affirmation. To exaggerate, to affirm, to resort to repetition, and never to attempt to prove anything by reasoning, are methods of argument well known to speakers at public meetings."

LeBon attributes special potency to the seduction of the audience by images,—to "the magic force of words and formulae, independent of their real sense." "The chief concern of a good counsel," he says, "should be to work upon the feelings of the jury, and, as with all crowds, to argue but little or only to employ rudimentary modes of reasoning."

We need not concern ourselves with the naïve explanations which this writer gives for the tendencies he attributes to all assemblages. It is clear that the composition of the "average audience" usually suffices to explain such phenomena when they actually occur. There is no necessity to invoke a "mental leveling," a "collective consciousness," a "brain paralysis," or "the unconsciousness of the mob."

The truth is that men are less different from each other in their physical make-up and anatomy, and in their original instinctive and emotional reactions, than they are in intelligence and wisdom, or in their acquired skills and standards. Men who agree in their repugnance to a given odor or their fear in danger may yet differ remarkably both in intelligence and knowledge. In so far as verdicts and acts relating to what LeBon calls "matters of general interest" are based on the fundamental interests, and such common inclinations as those toward mercy, justice, revenge, jealousy, pride, there is nothing either surprising or mysterious in the agreement of "the artist and the grocer." Their difference will lie rather in the type of object or situation most likely to arouse such reactions.

But the conception of the assembly as a mob which the speaker invariably seeks to stampede to some tumultous act or verdict, to be recalled perhaps with chagrin on the morrow or in history, is far from representing the audience or the enterprise which most speakers will confront. To present the frenzied and vociferous delivery of magical formulae, striking images, and seductive metaphors as the goal of public speaking is, to say the least, woefully to underestimate the varieties and occasions of public congregation.

MAJORITY VERSUS EXPERT OPINION

It is well known of course that individual opinion is influenced not only by strictly relevant data and personal evaluation, but also to a considerable extent by the suggestive influence of the opinions of others. The knowledge that the majority hold a given opinion inclines many individuals favorably toward the majority's decision. Similarly the verdict of an expert in the field in question gives a bias to the individual's judgment. Is the majority or the expert more potent in thus deflecting the individual opinion? Is the audience more susceptible, in general, to the statement of public opinion or to the quotation of authority?

In an experiment conducted in 1910, the writer attempted to measure the effectiveness of various types of appeal in the case of the description of marketable products. Among the thirty main interests or instincts represented were two which bear on the point just raised. Thus three appeals based their claim on the prestige of the group, thereby suggesting the desirability of the article. Two appeals, on the other hand, were based on the recommendations of prominent persons, who, in the public eye, might well represent expert opinion. If a perfect appeal, that is, one which for every member of the experimental group was the most effective of the series, be considered to have a value of 100 per cent, then, on this basis, the recommendation scores only 14 per cent whereas the Group Suggestion scores 50 per cent. The suggestion of the group is in this field apparently much more effective than is the opinion of the expert.

An experiment of H. T. Moore's [47] is directed toward a similar point. This investigator studied three types of situations; *viz.*, speech, morals, and music. "Ninety-five subjects were given eighteen paired comparisons for each of three types of situation. The instructions for the linguistic judgments were that the subjects check the more offensive one of each pair of expressions. . . . The ethical judgments involved the checking of the more offensive of two traits of character in each of eighteen pairs. . . . The musical judgments involved an expression of preference for one of two resolutions of the dominant seventh chord, played on a reed organ. Eighteen paired resolutions were played, and the preferences recorded after each."

After these opinions had been recorded and a time interval of several days had elapsed, a repetition of the experiment showed the chance of reversal for such judgments, when no suggestive influence was used. On later occasions this second half of the experiment was accompanied in each case by a statement of what the majority opinion had been on the original occasion. In a third case the statement was used instead of the opinion of some expert in the field of question. The investigator now inquired whether the suggestion of group opinion and of expert opinion produced a greater number of reversals of judgment than came by chance alone, and how these two influences compared in this respect, in the three fields of speech, morals, and music. The following tabulation of the results shows the outcome of this suggestive experiment.

FIELD OF JUDGMENT	REVERSALS WITHOUT SUGGESTION	REVERSALS UNDER SUGGESTION OF MAJORITY OPINION	REVERSALS UNDER SUGGESTION OF EXPERT OPINION
Speech . . .	13.4%	62.2%	48.0%
Morals . . .	10.3	50.1	47.8
Music . . .	25.1	48.2	46.2

It is clear from this table alone that both types of suggestion have a very real effect in producing reversal of the individual's previous judgments, in all three fields. But the figures cannot be compared directly, since the chance reversals in the three fields were not equally frequent. We may divide each value for the suggestive procedures by the chance result in the same field, and thus arrive at a more directly comparable statement of the strength of the two influences. This the investigator has done and the figures are as follows, using in each case the chance result as the unit.

FIELD OF JUDGMENT	INFLUENCE OF MAJORITY	INFLUENCE OF EXPERT
Speech	4.60	3.50
Morals	4.86	4.60
Music	1.90	1.80

The author concludes:

"If we now take as our unit of measurement the per cent recorded as the chance of reversal, we find, as indicated . . . that the probability of reversing favorably to the majority in matters of speech and morals in approximately five times chance; whereas in matters of musical feeling the probability is only about twice chance. By majority is meant here of course only the special type of majority provided in the experiment, but if generalization is permissible on the basis of the evidence available, we may venture the statement that a man is two and a half times as individualistic in his musical likes and dislikes as in his moral and linguistic perferences. Similarly we may conclude that expert and majority opinion hold about equal sway over the individual in morals and music, but that the chances are about ten to seven in favor of majority prestige in matters pertaining to speech."

An experiment similar to Moore's was more recently reported by Marple.[42a] Three groups of 300 subjects each were used, averaging respectively 18, 22, and 39 years of age. Opinions (Yes, No, Uncertain) were secured from all these on an array of 75 debatable propositions or questions. A month later opinions were again recorded, under the following three conditions:

A. Control Group—No suggestions offered.
B. Majority Opinion Influence—These subjects were now informed what the majority opinion had been on the earlier occasion.
C. Expert Opinion Influence—These subjects were now informed of the recorded opinion of 20 "experts."

The changes in the second opinion, to agree with the suggestive influence, were then computed. Two outstanding results appeared.

In the first place "whether measuring changes due to chance or those which occur in the presence of group or expert preference, there appears to be a decline of suggestibility with increasing age."

In the second place, "the influence of group preference in facilitating opinion is in every case greater than the influence of expert opinion."

The net outcome is consistent in all three of these investigations, and tends to indicate that, in the words of Marple, "Group opinion, with these groups, is more powerful in affecting individual agreement than is expert opinion."

Moore's concluding words, in pointing out the limitations of such an experiment, may also be given, as having relevance to the type of enterprise we are here undertaking. "Whether the shrunken prestige of a defeated political candidate or of an abdicated emperor follows any accurately describable laws, one would scarcely venture to say; but it is sufficiently obvious that until so-called social laws rest on more than the personal observations of individual writers, we shall have a great excess of laws and only a minimum of confidence in applying them."

THE DETERMINANTS OF BELIEF

In the long run the final test of belief is the readiness or the willingness to act. Indeed some psychologists have been convinced that the experience of belief is nothing more than the feeling of this readiness for action. However this may be, inducement to act must proceed either through relying on a belief explicitly or implicitly held, or else through the establishment of a new belief. Even the emotional appeal operates through the utilization of a native or long-acquired value, interest, preference, or conviction.

The psychology of arousing action thus involves in part the psychology of belief, and it would be useful in this connection to know what are the most effective determinants of our convictions. Such information would be of specially practical value in the endeavor to establish a new belief in the minds of one's audience, inasmuch as it would enable the speaker to take advantage of thought habits and lines of least resistance. Very little is known quantitatively or experimentally as to the relative potency of the different determinants of conviction, and this constitutes a field in which exploration will surely be profitable. It is unsafe to rely solely on anecdotal evidence, generalized clinical findings, and occasional striking or bizarre incidents, however instructive and suggestive these may be. Pending fuller experimental knowledge, the following account of a preliminary investigation of the determinants of belief in the case of educated adults has a significant value. All of the individuals studied were high-school graduates and all had had at least two years of college training in addition. The results thus apply to the most enlightened and reflective section of the population, and must not yet be taken as characterizing the average man.

Lund [42] presented to these thirty-five individuals a list of thirty propositions, presumably representing typical assertions in fields of general knowledge, science, ethics, politics, and religion. Each proposition was to be graded on a scale of belief. In each case also a statement was to be made of the determinants of the belief. The question was then, how firmly is this proposition believed, and what are the factors, influences, or determinants to which the direction and degree of belief is to be attributed.

The following propositions will serve as illustrations of the longer list, and will suggest the straightforwardness of the statements.

A. Were the higher forms of life derived from the lower forms through a gradual process of evolutionary growth?

B. Is the earth practically round?

C. Is morality a man-made institution?

D. Is the golden rule a practicable concept in business relations?

E. Is democracy the best form of government?

F. Is the protective tariff a wise policy for the United States?

G. Did Shakespeare write *The Merchant of Venice*?

H. Is slander wrong?

I. Does death end personal existence?

J. Does a black cat crossing your path bring bad luck?

The scale ratings ranged from a neutral attitude to very high degrees of belief or disbelief; beliefs in different fields displayed varying degrees of certainty; and numerous other interesting tendencies were observed. But our present interest is instead in the nature of the determining influences cited as responsible for the degree of belief. By these we do not mean "arguments" that might be given for or against the proposition, but instead the candid report of the presumed influences underlying or leading to the conviction.

These "determinants" (1050 indications, 30 from each of 35 individuals) were classified, independently, or in consultation, by a group of 20 college students of psychology, in an experimental course. It was found that ten categories adequately took account of such classification as could be made. The designations of these categories, and the frequency with which they occurred in the total number of "determinants" cited, are given in the following table.

DETERMINANTS	FREQUENCIES
A—Teaching and training	326
B—Personal experience	151
C—Personal opinion	116
D—Personal reasoning	92
E—Desire and satisfyingness	58
F—Authoritative opinion	46
G—Public opinion	44
H—Axiomatic principle	6
(Individual responses)	125
(No response)	86
TOTAL	1050

Such results will no doubt vary with different groups of individuals and with differently chosen propositions, and they will depend also on the degree of conscious insight which individuals actually have into the grounds of their convictions and the process of forming them. But if these data are typical, they show that the appeals to emotional satisfaction, to authoritative and crowd opinion, and to unsupported acceptance are reported as much less accredited than are more reflective and empirical considerations, and that most accredited of all are the habits of thought established through the long process of training and teaching.

Of course the accrediting of a determinant is not a demonstration that that factor was actually operative in shaping the individual belief. It is however an indication of the probable esteem in which the individual holds the determinant,—an indication of his own belief concerning the determination of his beliefs. An interesting feature of Lund's investigation consisted in requiring his subjects also to rate these determinants as they supposed them to apply to the average individual of their social and educational status. The noteworthy result was that the more rational determinants were indicated as being more potent for each individual in his own case than he supposed them to be for people at large.

We have already shown how close is the correlation between the satisfyingness of a proposition's content and its degree of belief strength. The present result shows that in general, although we are inclined to attribute this non-rational determination to the beliefs of others, we suppose ourselves to be more rationally guided. It is in part this inclination which leads the average man to welcome evidence, but to be satisfied with the fallacious modes of proof. For this is enough to enable conviction, which springs from desire, to possess the appearance of cogent rational support.

PRACTICAL CONCLUSIONS

1. The first principle for directing the acts and verdicts of the audience is that of indicating specifically and definitely rather than vaguely and generally the precise nature, place, time, and method of the proposed act.

2. The strength of a suggestion varies directly with its spontaneity, vividness, positive form, prestige, and frequency.

3. The strength of a suggestion varies inversely with the internal resistance it encounters and with the number of rival suggestions operating.

4. Repetition with variation promotes conviction; repetition with duplication better specifies and defines the response to be made.

5. A slogan or catch-word crystallizes a whole program and remains with the audience as a succinct formula of action.

6. If audiences are more easily aroused to malicious than to ennobling acts or verdicts, this is in part because anger, hate, and fear are emotions most easily recognized in others and propagated through their demeanor.

7. The mobilization of an audience depends no more upon the actions of the leader than upon the contributory signs afforded one another by the auditors, through their attitudes and visible expressions.

8. The traditional "mental inferiority of all congregations" is only a result of the fact that people are more alike in the simple, primitive, concrete structural, and fundamental traits than they are in complex, more recently acquired, symbolic, functional, and derived traits.

9. The prevalent "mob conception" of the nature of an audience woefully underestimates the varieties and occasions of public congregation.

10. There is no "mind of the audience"; there are only the individual people with their individual minds; but in a congregation special stimuli and hence special behavior occur which are absent when the individuals are alone.

11. Whether the opinion of the public or the judgment of experts has higher prestige with an audience, varies with the subject matter of the discourse.

12. People prefer their acts to appear rationally determined; they suppose their own acts to be more rationally determined than the acts of others; they suppose their own acts to be more rationally determined than they actually are.

CHAPTER X

THE AUDITORIUM

ARCHITECTURAL FEATURES

Not the least important of those factors conspiring to win an audience is the auditorium itself. Numerous suggestions might be made here, some of which are entirely obvious and commonplace. It is nevertheless true that in spite of their obviousness many of these factors are commonly ignored, with disastrous results.

Whenever possible, the speaker should choose the auditorium, bearing in mind quite specifically the purpose and character of his appeal. The architectural features, which determine in the main the acoustics of the room, are usually beyond his control, and the discussion of accoustics is a problem not for the psychologist first, but for the builder. But the speaker will, if it is not possible to visit the room beforehand and thus to make sure of its characteristics in these respects by trying out his voice, at least pay careful attention to this matter in the very beginning of his discourse. He will have learned, from those whose specialty this is, or from his own experience, how to adjust his speaking voice to the size of the room, the distance of the audience, and how to make his words intelligible without inducing strain or effort either on his own part or on that of his auditors.

But the size or shape of the room, the distance and elevation of the platform, the seating arrangements, the previous uses of the auditorium, its illumination and ventilation, involve specific psychological reactions as well. The favorableness or unfavorableness of these details will vary with the purpose and nature of the occasion.

THE INFLUENCE OF PHYSICAL ARRANGEMENT

That the physical character and arrangement of the room has a demonstrable influence on the mental processes of its occupants is more than an occult fancy, and it has been experimentally demonstrated by Brown and Wong.[7] These investigators prepared two rooms, of similar size, and both sufficiently illuminated for the purpose of the experiment. Two groups of subjects were used, 12 in each group. These two groups of individuals were so similar in intellectual ability that the average scores on the Army Alpha Test differed by only about 3 points out of 136, in the two groups.

One experimental room was "filled with old apparatus, lumber, chairs, clothes, cases of old bottles in disorder, odds and ends" and "particular pains were taken to have this material clutter the floor at each side of the subject's seat so that whenever his eyes left the ugly screen in front of him they fell upon these disorderly objects."

The other experimental room was well furnished and trimmed, carpeted, with book cases, pictures, and vases; the screen, instead of being an ugly and roughly lettered piece of cardboard from a packing box, was neatly covered with green felt cloth. "The whole effect was orderly and restrained and, in the opinion of the writers, pleasing."

A complicated piece of mental work, based on the "multiple choice method" of the psychological laboratory, was set for both groups. The task was the same, the work was done at the same time of day, and under the same general conditions, except for the orderliness and disorderliness of the two experimental rooms. None of the subjects knew the true purpose of the experiment, but all were instructed to do the best work they could so as to test their ability to solve problems and to learn more about their mental processes.

The mental work accomplished by the two groups was then compared. It was found that the groups working in an orderly auditorium accomplished 39 per cent more mental work than did the group working under conditions of disorder. Under the orderly conditions (*1*) more problems were solved; (*2*) fewer trials were required for a problem; (*3*) fewer false reactions were made per problem; (*4*) less time was required for the solution of a problem; and (*5*) the work was less random in character.

The following table of results shows the quantitative measures reported by these two investigators.

	"Disorderly" Average	"Orderly" Average	"Orderly" Superiority
No. of problems solved . .	5.5	7.7	2.2
No. of trials per problem . .	41.0	31.2	9.8
No. of reactions per problem .	136.6	102.0	34.6
No. of trials in 100 minutes .	197.8	254.6	56.8
No. of reactions in 100 minutes	672.2	802.0	129.8
No. of reactions per trial . .	3.4	3.1	.3

More detailed analysis of these results, and statements of the reliability of the averages and the differences are given by the investigators, who have also used other types of mental work under the same sets of conditions. They conclude, in general that, "The effect of working in a disorderly room is materially to reduce the number of problems solved and the quality of the work of solution."

It would be interesting to know somewhat more specifically in just what way these unfavorable physical surroundings operated. Did they distract the workers' attention by deflecting it to the foreign objects? Did they induce a general feeling of unpleasantness and discomfort which then interfered with the effective progress of mental work? Did they perhaps, by way of "empathy," set up inco-ordination and disorder in the general adjustments which the work involved? Or was it perhaps instead the favorable surroundings that operated, by inducing more than the average attitudes and feelings of comfort, well being, and harmony, and thus indirectly suggesting high standards of accomplishment?

On these points the experiment does not inform us. But as it stands it is sufficiently instructive for our purpose, for it shows unmistakably that the physical arrangement, contents, and disposition of a room may very materially influence the mental processes of its occupants, and there is no reason for supposing that this is any less true of the auditorium than it is of the workroom.

SEATING ARRANGEMENTS

If the speaker is interested in welding together, mentally, the members of his audience, for purposes of enthusiasm and concerted feeling, it is important to realize that spiritual sympathy is promoted by physical proximity. Students of crowd psychology lay great stress on the influence of the consciousness of the bodily nearness of associates and fellows. Thus Scott,[60] in considering the various ways of securing homogeneity in a group of individuals, writes, "One of the most helpful methods is to get the audience to sit close together. It is easy to speak to a packed house, but it would take a Demosthenes to make an impression when separated from his audience by a yawning abyss of empty seats. Five hun-

dred people scattered over an auditorium which seats
three thousand can scarcely be welded into a homogeneous audience, while the same individuals crowded into a
room which is intended but for four hundred are easily
changed into a psychological crowd. This fact forces
itself on all public speakers and leads them to attempt to
have only certain groups of seats occupied and preferably
the front ones in order that the vacant ones may not
form a barrier between the speaker and the hearers. The
touching of elbows adds to the consciousness of the presence of others in a way that cannot be secured in any
other way."

Obviously the principle may be applied in the reverse
way as well. If the speaker contemplates a logical appeal
to the intelligence of his auditors rather than to their
imitative suggestiveness or to their emotions, he will do
well to secure reasonable segregation of his individual
hearers, with undistracted opportunity for personal polarization toward the speaker alone.

THE INFLUENCE OF DISTRACTIONS

One who has tried to conduct a prayer meeting, to lead
a discussion on sex hygiene, or to lecture on psycho-
pathology in a room invaded by distracting noises from
the outside well knows the psychology involved in seeking to control such intruding factors. Their competition
for the attention of the audience is the least important
of their influences, though one by no means to be disre-
garded. There is for many topics an appropriate or at
least a conventional mode of speech. Political contro-
versy and vituperative propaganda can often be shouted
without loss of power, but matters of serious moment,
topics bearing closely on the personal life of individuals,
matters involving close distinction, and appeals directed

to the calmer reflection or the aesthetic sensibility often require for their adequate expression a voice pitched in the lower ranges of intensity.

VENTILATION

Faulty ventilation of the auditorium is in many cases responsible in part for the sleepiness and stupor of the audience. Superstitions about ventilation may readily lead to false steps in this direction. That being confined in a crowded and poorly ventilated room produces drowsiness, lassitude, and even headache is a common observation. But these discomforts, which so interfere with the winning of the audience, have been found by experiment not to come from the chemical constitution of the air, low oxygen content, high carbon dioxide content, "crowd poison," in even extraordinary and experimental conditions. Instead, these effects seem to come essentially from the temperature and the humidity of the air.

The bodies of the auditors are constantly producing more heat than is necessary for maintaining their normal temperature, as the result of muscular, nervous, and glandular activity. The excess is given off partly by way of the warm expired air, and partly and in the main by radiation from the surface of the body and by evaporation of the perspiration thrown out upon the skin by the sweat glands. These processes of radiation and evaporation depend not only upon the condition of the body but also upon the condition of the atmosphere surrounding it. If the temperature of the air is higher than that of the body, radiation from body to air would not occur. Instead the opposite exchange would take place. Further, if the air is saturated with moisture, evaporation from the body cannot take place. The body may thus easily suffer from overheating, and it is this overheating that causes the lassitude, drowsiness, and headache. Temperature and humidity of the air in the auditorium are therefore the two most important factors to be considered, and the two must always be considered in connection with each other. The optimum humidity increases with increase of temperature.

With the occupants at rest, the most satisfactory temperature for lecture halls and auditoriums is from 61 to 64 Fahrenheit. With the temperature of 68, the humidity should be about 60. The wet-bulb thermometer gives a record of temperature and humidity combined, and a reading of 60 on such a thermometer is recommended by ventilating engineers. Inclosed air should be kept in motion by fans or by a current of air from an open window. Driving the overheated air from the surface of the body promotes evaporation and reduces the temperature of the body.

ILLUMINATION

Aside from sufficient light for the purposes of the occasion, the great desideratum in the illumination of the auditorium is the prevention of glare from sources of light placed directly in the visual field of the audience. Such sources of light not only produce undue eye strain and fatigue, with accompanying sleepiness or discomfort, but they act as constant centers of distraction. Reflexly, the eye tends to turn toward these bright spots and either attention is thus drawn from the speaker or else the auditor must make constant effort to resist the reflex tendency. It is less important to have a high intensity of light, for ordinary purposes than it is to have evenness of illumination. The eye readily adapts itself to different light intensities, and under conditions of uniform distribution the absolute intensity of the light within a wide range has little effect on the clearness of vision. Evenly distributed illumination such as is produced by daylight and by properly installed indirect artificial lighting gives the best results. If these are not available, the only resource is to seek by simple means to approximate the effect as closely as possible, by such devices as reducing the absolute intensity at the source, shading the eyes from the direct source of light, or putting shades upon these sources.

Illumination is of course to be considered not only from the point of view of clarity and comfort of vision, but also for its influence on the general feelings and mood of the audience. Among the numerous things that arouse in us, either natively or as the result of occasional or frequent experience, particular emotions and attitudes, are the various degrees of brightness and the array of colors. Depending on the purpose of the assemblage, considerable suggestive use of illumination can be made so as indirectly to induce the mood or frame of mind appropriate to the topic. In churches and theaters this use of effective illumination has developed into a fine art. An early recognition and attempt to formulate some of the laws is to be found in Burke's "Essay on the Sublime and Beautiful":[10]

"I think then, that all edifices calculated to produce an idea of the sublime, ought rather to be dark and gloomy, and this for two reasons: the first is, that darkness itself on other occasions is known by experience to have a greater effect on the passions than light. The second is, that to make an object very striking, we should make it as different as possible from the objects with which we have been immediately conversant; when therefore you enter a building, you cannot pass into a greater light than you had in the open air; to go into one some few degrees less luminous can only make a trifling change; but to make the transition thoroughly striking, you ought to pass from the greatest light to as much darkness as is consistent with the uses of architecture. At night the contrary rule will hold, but for the very same reason; and the more highly a room is then illuminated, the grander will the passion be."

THE PLATFORM

The disposition of the platform and its elevation is another mechanical feature not to be ignored. The platform not only renders the speaker more easily visible to the whole audience, but in doing this it also sets him apart from them, gives a formal touch to their relation, more definitely polarizing the audience toward him. The elimination of the platform not only puts the speaker on the same physical level with the audience but also tends to make him part of it or at least more intimately related to it. In general, the larger the audience, the more formal the theme, and the more difficult the task of control is expected to be, the more useful will the platform be found. Obviously also, if the speaker is to utilize graphic materials, charts, or other visual aids, the elevated platform will possess the advantages of better display.

Another suggestion of a psychological sort, perhaps somewhat far-fetched, has been made concerning the use of the platform in public assemblages. Part of the performer's task is to increase the suggestibility of the audience, that is, to bring them into more effective *rapport* with him. Now one of the most suggestible moments for people in general is the condition of drowsiness. The psychotherapist takes advantage of this by introducing his suggestions when the patient is in a half-waking, or sleepy condition. Sometimes this condition is deliberately induced by artificial means, such as bright light, monotonous sounds, and other devices. It is even possible that a certain tractableness which characterizes night audiences as distinguished from the restlessness of day-time assemblies is due to the greater sleepiness, and hence the readier suggestibility then prevalent. At least, experiments have shown that in that type of suggestibility that is involved in laboratory "illusions" the effectiveness of the illusion is greater in the evening than in the morning.

In going to sleep, it has been pointed out, the eyes normally turn upward. Moreover, one of the favorite means of inducing the "hypnagogic" or sleepy state is to cause the subject fixedly to look at a small object, placed somewhat above the level of the eyes in looking straight ahead. Now this is one of the effects of the platform. It causes the members of the audience to turn their eyeballs slightly upward, somewhat as they normally do in falling asleep. If this position brings with it, or tends to bring with it a slight drowsiness, favorable to suggestibility and *rapport,* the use of the platform would appear to have a psychological as well as a mechanical advantage.

PRACTICAL CONCLUSIONS

1. The architectural features, physical arrangement, contents, disposition, previous uses, and associations of the auditorium exert measureable influences on the mental processes that go on within it.

2. Social sympathy is promoted by physical closeness, which therefore favors the emotional appeal; logical persuasion is better encouraged by separating the members of the audience more widely.

3. Faulty ventilation and illumination often escape the blame which the performer unjustly bears.

4. Uniformity of illumination is as important as brightness, and indirect lighting prevents reflex wandering of the eye and consequent distraction and discomfort.

5. The larger the audience, the more formal the themes and the more difficult the task of control, the more useful is the platform as an auditorium adjunct.

6. Elevation of the performer above the floor level favors his prestige and often gives added influence to his suggestions; dispensing with the platform, on the other hand, favors that mode of *rapport* in which the audience takes a strong initiative.

CHAPTER XI

THE INFLUENCE OF THE AUDIENCE

INDIVIDUAL REACTIONS

Discussions of the audience usually concern themselves with the reaction of the group to the individual. Only in the case of "mobs" and "crowds" is the reaction of the individual to the group commonly considered. But any speaker who recalls his early platform experiences is likely to realize that even the most orderly, friendly, and dispassionate audience exerts a tremendous influence on the individual who has the temerity to confront it. Among the numerous familiar fears of mankind none is more common than "stage fright." Teachers no less than pupils experience stage fright. Public performers of almost every kind may suffer from it. Even animals lower than man appear to be influenced by the presence and attitude of spectators.

Nor are the effects of the audience entirely due to inexperience, youth, or unpreparedness. Among many very simple factors which produce characteristic reactions on the part of even the most seasoned performer are such things as the size, arrangement, familiarity, composition, and attitude of the audience. Years of experience on the public platform often fail to bring immunity to stage fright. The reactions thus produced may often amount to acute bodily distress. We may very well inquire, then, in what various ways the audience acts upon the speaker or other performer, and what psychological factors underlie this influence.

THE HUMAN NEED FOR AN AUDIENCE

In the first place, most human beings demand an audience or spectators, at least in their childhood and youth, and ordinarily throughout their lives. Juvenile accomplishment is strongly spurred by the presence and approval of an audience. Mere infants often prove exasperating by their insistence on making their mud pies or snow men out in front of a group of adults, rather than around the corner or behind the benches. "See me! See me," is the cry when almost any trivial accomplishment is staged.

And it is apparent also that not only is the audience desired as a witness, attesting to the fact of youthful accomplishment. Often enough the very initial motive to the act is seen to come from the presence of spectators and the chance thus given to appear to good advantage before some one. The charm of the act fades away when the auditors or spectators fail to play their role.

If perchance the motivation of the performance lay elsewhere, no sooner is success achieved than the clamor for an audience arises; and it is not easy to make sure to what extent the possibility of such exhibitionism was a factor in the original incentive. "All the world's a stage," indeed, but a stage alone would never lead us to act; for that, the credit usually must go to the audience before which the stage is set.

In juveniles this passion for an audience is commonly called "showing off." It is so strong a motive in the young that the elders often seek to moderate, suppress, or punish it. Beyond the days of childhood the same impulse asserts itself in the exhibitionism and affectation of the youth. In adult life the longing for display persists; titles, distinctions, uniforms, fads and fashions, monuments and ceremonials give to it a kind of social sanction and machinery.

Concern over facial and sartorial appearance, over physical stigmata, over dress and address, personal accomplishment and disability, reveal the typical adolescent as living consciously among "a cloud of witnesses." The courting impulse, now actively at work, lends further vigor to the "instinct of display." But display does not cease when the personnel of domestic partnerships is decided. Instead, the very decision itself must be flaunted before the audience and heralded abroad. The personalities concerned each rejoice in the favorable publicity and effective exhibit of the chosen one. The wedding seems inadequate unless it is staged before an audience.

THE FUNCTION OF THE AUDIENCE

Advertising as an enterprise is not limited to the promotion of commercial commodities or services. Throughout the coquetry and courtship of animals, the antics and escapades of children, the debut, promenade and haberdashery of youth, the emblems of heraldry, the tournaments, festivals, balls, and banquets of the leisured, and even through the splendid tortures of the saints, can be traced the passion for an audience. "Conspicuous waste," indeed, has been effectively argued to be the key to such social phenomena as style and fashion, and the conspicuous inevitably involves spectators or an audience.

Even the sober achievements of men of science, of artists, explorers, writers, have their own degree of dependence on the desire of individual workers to appear to good advantage before some audience. Humanity's servitors usually see to it that their names and addresses are announced; recognition is, in many serious endeavors, as effective a reward as wages.

Without an audience, women relapse and men become unkempt. However near cleanliness may be to divinity, the immaculate habits of civilization are dictated no more by the bodily comfort and hygiene of the individual than by "what people will say." Indeed, one of the gravest signs of mental disorder is that loss of contact with reality in which the patient's conduct is no longer guided by its relation to his audience. Deny to art and science, to commerce, politics, and war, the stimulus of the audience, and rare indeed would be the worker whose industry would not slump. Perhaps the most significant things about a man's character are the locus, size, personnel, and quality of the audience that motivates his conduct and the degree to which these factors are explicitly formulated in his own consciousness.

Not only is apathy toward one's accustomed audience or social setting a probable sign of grave changes in the organization of personality; the loss of this audience may in turn induce just such profound alterations, and may incline the individual toward mental instability. A man who had been throughout his life a Methodist preacher reached the age of superannuation and was retired from his charge. He lost the audience before which his whole adult life had been shaped, and in terms of which his thought and feeling had been organized. The loss was not easily met. At first there was restlessness, vague uneasiness, querulousness, and varied signs of distress. Then the "lost" orator began to write regular sermons, as had been his former habit. But the mere writing of sermons was inadequate,—they demanded an audience. He thereupon proceeded to read his sermons to his family, from week to week, or oftener.

In this bit of mental hygiene the family did not whole-heartedly co-operate. Instead, they sought diligently to substitute a surrogate activity, to sublimate, as it were, the lost orator's hunger for listeners. They set him to work painting all the household furniture, hoping that this would distract his mind from his trouble, and rescue the newly found family audience. They were disappointed. In the twinkling of an eye the furniture had all been painted, feverishly, in order to get back to the familiar activity. In despair the family decided that the painting job was unsatisfactory, the colors were all wrong, and insisted that all the furniture be scraped, cleaned, and again repainted.

This outcome suggests quite clearly that it was not mere want of occupation that constituted the source of personal aggravation and mental distress on the part of the old man. Occupation was present in abundance. It was not even the loss of the accustomed occupation, for no objection was expressed to the free writing of sermons, and this could have been indulged in with no complaint. No, the thing that made the old man a problem of social maladjustment was his demand for an audience. It was not enough merely to be active, nor even actively to express one's thoughts. The activity must be observed, the thoughts must be listened to. Preferably, they must be applauded or at least recognized. The therapeutic salvation in such a case would of course have been not to set miscellaneous "busy work" for the old gentleman, but to urge him to write sermons for publication, in a book which, it might at least be suggested, would secure for his performance an even larger audience than that of his accustomed congregation. Diverting, rather than suppressing an urge, always has a therapeutic advantage.

THE GREGARIOUS INSTINCT

Social psychologists and sociologists have made much of the supposed gregarious instinct of human beings. The reality of such an innate need as mere company is very doubtful. Recall that the human infant is born to and among other people, that throughout the long period of infancy it is the center of a solicitous and admiring audience. The social heritage into which it enters in home, school, and work constantly sets it as an individual over against society as an audience. We should not be surprised then to find such an individual lonesome in solitude, and inclined to frequent the places where others congregate. Social heritage makes actors of us all, and in the absence of the audience we feel a loss very like that of the smoker who has lost his pipe. But are the pangs of the former any more innate and instinctive than those of the latter? The evidence for such a conclusion is far from convincing. The addiction to an audience, acquired through the prolonged adaptation to the presence of spectators, may indeed be all that underlies the supposed "gregarious instinct."

TYPICAL AUDIENCE EFFECTS

If then we live always in a cloud of witnesses, and if the actuality or hope of an audience motivates so much of human conduct, why should we be so nervous when first addressing a public assembly, and why do most of us remain so throughout our lives? How are we to explain those profound organic disturbances, affecting the poise and motor control, the pulse and vaso-motor mechanisms, the glands of the body, the digestive tract, and the neuro-muscular tonus of the whole system, so often experienced by one who appears before an audience?

Apparently much depends upon the type of audience, not so much upon its degree of polarization, but instead upon the spatial and temporal relations of the audience to the performer. The writer, explorer, and artist act, in the main, for the sake of a remote audience, either in space or in time. The achievement, however motivated by exhibitionism it may be, is actually performed away from the audience, which in fact exists only after the feat is accomplished. Immediate spectators and companions or co-workers may indeed be present, but these comprise a minor and secondary audience, of a different type. If such spectators should be numerous, and expressly recognized as observers, we then have an audience in the more common sense of the term,—a group of witnesses bodily present and explicitly in the consciousness of the performer.

Such an audience reacts in more or less complex fashion on most individuals. Other things aside, the reaction depends on the native temperament and the experience of the performer, the nature of the occasion, and the attitude of the audience. At one extreme the individual is moved by the audience to greater endeavor and activity. Co-ordinations run smoothly, enthusiasm is high, and a sense of personal power is felt. The focus of attention is the audience, and the details of performance fall into the background of consciousness. No doubt a physiologist could show that the pleasurable excitement involved so affects the sympathetic nervous system as to release new stores of blood-sugar into the system, thus affording unwonted energy, vitality, and confidence. Such an individual is stimulated by the presence of spectators to superior performance, and shows to best advantage in the limelight. In psychoses of the extremely extrovert form, the presence of spectators readily sets going the flow of speech or the press of activity which constitutes the external aspect of the clinical picture.

Interesting observations on the effect of an audience have been made in the study of stuttering. Individuals are not infrequently found who in private conversation stutter very badly. Or as students in a classroom they stutter when called upon to recite or to address the instructor. But the same individuals who manifest this distressing handicap may be confident and fluent public speakers before an audience. Indeed, they may themselves be successful teachers of younger or less well-informed students, and exhibit no speech defects in the classroom. It is said that several public orators with distinguished records of success as speakers suffer from stuttering in their private communication.

Various suggestions have been offered by way of explanation of such facts. Thus it has been suggested that loud speaking facilitates the stutterer, and that public address thus favors him. Or it has been surmised that just as the stutterer may sing without difficulty, when a rhythm is thus extraneously imposed upon his speech, so his frequent rehearsals of his speech give it an automatic character which his spontaneous conversation lacks. Perhaps the most suggestive explanation is that which calls attention to the difference in the social situation. The speaker, by virtue of his position and right of way, is afforded a certain elation, a mild social status of superiority for the moment, just as the teacher has a prestige which the pupils lack. Given this added buoyancy of confidence, the usual fear of speech inadequacy drops away. But the experience of stage fright shows very well that not every one's speech is facilitated by the audience situation.

At the other extreme is the individual who is much

less in need of an audience, and who is inhibited, confused, and handicapped when he stands before one. His own acts and thoughts may in themselves have adequate interest for him, but the presence of others sets up inhibitions, doubts, mild fears, and insecurities, provokes shyness rather than sociability and display as a typical picture. Either the audience, or the task in hand, or the performer's own person and position, or all of these together, become conspicuous objects of attention. The extrovert attends to his task or to his audience, as the occasion requires, taking the other for granted in each case, and his bodily self is likely to be more or less marginal in consciousness, if conscious at all. But the introvert, faced with the audience, is painfully conscious of himself as well and may attempt conscious control of acts that are ordinarily automatic. He can take nothing for granted, and in the face of all three objects of attention interference, error, trepidation, and anxiety appear, with manifest bodily symptoms.

There is perhaps a knack in regarding the audience as if it were a unit, which is often acquired only through practice and experience. Ordinary communication is between individuals. But in facing the audience the performer must compromise between two possibilities,—that of relating himself to the group as a whole, as a photographer would, or that of directing his attention to particular individuals in it. This compromise, in which some elements of both attitudes blend or alternate, is one of the most comfortable and reassuring things for the speaker to acquire. Until he acquires it his vocal utterance, bearing, and gesture, as well as the flow of his thought, are likely to be insecure and to miscarry.

That the attitude of the audience is an effective determiner of the speaker's reactions is a well recognized fact.

But it is far from easy to specify precisely what this effect will be, since it varies with the performer, and with the same performer from time to time. The apathetic and inert audience that chills the zeal of one speaker will fire another with strenuous determination to "get a rise out of them before it is over." The unfriendly or belligerent audience that intimidates one will excite another to a heightened aggressiveness. The responsive and applauding audience that strikes new sparks in the mind of one speaker may provoke another to relax his effort and to resort to easy expedients and cheap ideas. In just such a fashion the antics of children may degenerate into silliness before spectators who are unduly responsive.

THE NEED FOR MORE EXACT DATA

Attempts to explain these differences in individual reactions are likely to be specious. It is likely to be said, for example, that how the speaker will react to the audience depends on his particular instinctive equipment. If the "instinct of aggressiveness" is in him more conspicuously developed than is the "instinct of submission," or vice versa, it may be said, characteristic reactions will be found. If shyness overbalances sociability, if introversion is stronger than extroversion, etc., definite behavior will result. As a matter of fact the invocation of these "instincts" is far from explanation. Indeed the "instincts" are inferred only on the basis of the characteristic reactions, and the instincts are only names for these characteristic modes of response. But to invoke the name of a thing as an explanation of it is not likely to promote genuine understanding.

The generalities invoked up to this point and the frequent appeal to what is "well known" or "obvious," signify, actually, only a lack of exact knowledge. Few careful and precise studies seem to have been made of the actual effect of definite audiences on particular individuals. Hence here, as in the case of our other topics, no scientific psychology of the audience exists. Only somewhat preliminary attempts to apply exact methods to the problem may be reported here, by way of suggesting the type of inquiry that might be extended to significant and instructive proportions.

PRACTICAL CONCLUSIONS

1. Stage fright is a common human experience, and the individual afflicted with it need not feel that he is in this respect peculiar or abnormal.

2. The realization that all human beings crave an audience will promote a sympathetic understanding of much human behavior.

3. One of the primary functions of an audience is to give assurance and inspiration to the performer.

4. The loss of a lifetime audience is best adjusted to, not by suppression of the exhibitionist urge but by diverting this impulse into new directions.

5. The gregarious impulse in men is probably not an inherited instinct but instead an outcome of the social settings into which they are born.

6. The striking paradox for the psychologist is the joint activity of two opposing impulses,—craving for an audience and fear of it.

7. The extrovert welcomes the audience and is stimulated by its presence; the introvert may yearn for the audience but is inhibited by its presence.

8. The audience is not a unit, but it is often useful for the beginner to confront it as if it were.

9. Individual differences in reaction to an audience are often to be explained by past successes or failures of the individual before such groups.

CHAPTER XII

EXPERIMENTAL STUDIES OF AUDIENCE EFFECTS

EARLY INVESTIGATIONS

In a paper on "The Group as a Stimulus to Mental Activity," Burnham [9] raised the question,—"What is the effect on mental activity of the presence of a group of other persons, if studied objectively like the effects of temperature, barometric pressure, and the like?" In this paper he gives also a survey of the studies of the influence of the group upon the individual's performance and conduct. Although these early studies occupied themselves with the effect of co-workers mainly, the problem is sufficiently related to the one we are here concerned with for it to be worth while reviewing the results of earlier studies.

Several experiments have been conducted for the purpose of comparing the quantity and quality of achievement of individuals working in solitude and the same individuals working in the presence of others, or working jointly with others. Although the performer-audience relation has not usually been stressed in these cases, similar influences are probably at work in all sorts of group situations. The individual in the presence of fellow workers or spectators is actuated by motives that are absent in solitude. Most of the experiments to be reported from the earlier investigations have related to the work of children and students, and they do not involve that more or less voluntary reduction of achievement to the level of the poorest worker in the group that is sometimes found in adult group labor.

WORKING ALONE AND IN GROUPS

Mayer [9] set such tasks as mental and written arithmetic, dictation, memory tests, and verbal completion exercises, to twenty-eight schoolchildren, averaging twelve years of age. When working in groups, the performance was superior to that accomplished by the same pupils working alone. With this type of work the gain appeared not only in the time required but also in the quality of the work done, under the instruction to work both quickly and well.

Triplett [9] studied the effect of a single co-worker on a simple motor performance,—turning a reel at maximum speed. The presence of a co-worker resulted, in general, in more rapid work. But in the case of some individuals hasty and inco-ordinated movements were produced, which rendered the work inferior. This effect is similar to that of such a drug as caffein on certain types of performance, such as discrimination reaction. The effect of the drug is in general stimulation. But stimulation, in a process calling for discrimination, may result in faulty judgment and impetuous reaction, which, since accuracy is part of the requirement, eventually lead to slower work in the effort to eliminate mistakes.

Various observers have recorded the stimulating effect of the presence of a witness, especially in the case of muscular work. If the companion is a competing fellow worker, he serves the purpose of pacemaker, provoking rivalry and greater effort. This effect of course is not quite like that of an audience or witness, so far as the external circumstances are concerned. But the underlying psychological mechanisms are probably the same in both cases,—a new incentive is offered, appealing to the motive of display or pride and perhaps inducing a mild excitement that is favorable to livelier activity. Individual differences may be supposed to depend in part at least upon the relative amount of these two influences, since overexcitement may lead to inferior performance, in spite of the accompanying incentive.

Meumann [9] has also shown in experiments with school children that "In case of the test of the pupils separately, with no one else in the room, the amount of work was always less than when others were present." This was found both for muscular work, using the dynamometer and the ergograph, and for tests of memory for disconnected words. Burnham, in referring to these early studies, remarks that "the weight of evidence thus far seems to indicate the advantage of group work, except when individual and original thinking is required. . . . There are also undoubtedly, great individual differences as regards the effect of social environment; there are even perhaps different types as regards the effectiveness of the stimuli from the social group."

These early studies at least suggest the considerable variety of influences that may be operative in the effect of an audience. We may see even in these preliminary experiments, the effect of excitement, the influence of new or increased incentive, of affective and emotional attitudes, of pacemaking, of rivalry and display, and the compensatory arousal of greater energy usually provoked by mild distractions. One of the most interesting results of experiments on the conditions of effective work is the frequent finding that the introduction of distractions and obstacles often results in better rather than in poorer work. In all of these ways the audience may function, as well as in other ways not exhibited in these simple investigations of the work of schoolchildren.

Thus F. H. Allport [2] studied the work of a considerable number of college students when working alone and when working in groups of four or five members. The processes chiefly studied were those of free chain association and the writing of critical arguments. A variety of experiments were undertaken, which cannot be readily brought together in a summary table. But the chief tendencies were as follows.

Working in the presence of the group clearly resulted in greater speed in the process of free association. This result was more striking when every word occurring in a chain of associations was written than when only every third or fourth word was written. The influence of the group thus seems to have been more favorable for the motor and mechanical process of writing than for the more strictly mental processes of thinking of the words. Inferior performers showed the favorable effect of the group more clearly than did better workers, and other individual differences in susceptibility were shown. From the point of view of speed or quantity of work, then, the influence of the group was stimulating,—free association chains ran their course more rapidly, in the case of from seventy to ninety per cent of the individuals. Various other interesting quantitative changes were suggested, but not conclusively demonstrated,—such as the tendency for the beneficial effect to be more conspicuous in the earlier part of the work period than later on, and for the variability of individuals from one another to increase under the group influence.

In the writing of critical arguments against epigrams

from Epictetus and Marcus Aurelius, more ideas were also produced under the group conditions, and there was a general tendency toward greater wordiness,—thought tended to be expansive rather than intensive. But when the ideas were rated according to their logical value, the ideas produced under group conditions were found to be of an inferior value. Ideas of superior logical quality were more frequent under conditions of solitary work.

The writer reports that other experiments of his, upon the influence of a social setting on attention and on mental work, agree with these results, in that "the social influence was found to improve the quantity but not the quality of the mental performance."

In a later account of his experiments Allport [3] gives a detailed examination of the results, with a number of extremely suggestive interpretations. The results are also briefly summarized in the following words:

"The social stimulations present in the co-acting group bring about an increase in the speed and quantity of work produced by the individual. This increase is more pronounced in work involving overt, physical movements than in purely intellectual tasks. In adults the group produces no improvement in the constancy of attention or the quality of the work performed. Some individuals in fact do inferior work in the presence of co-workers. There is a lowering of the logical value of reasoning carried out in the group; but an increase in the number of words by which such reasoning is expressed. . . . The social increment is subject to individual differences in respect to age, ability, and personality traits. It is greatest for the least able workers and least for the most able."

Allport cites two processes in explanation of these accelerating effects. One is the stimulating influence of rivalry. The other is social facilitation through the fact that "the movements made by others performing the same task as ourselves serve as contributory stimuli, and increase or hasten our own responses."

The experiments cited up to this point, although they have to do with the presence of other people, are not strictly relevant to our topic, since the other people, in these experiments, have been fellow workers rather than spectators or auditors. In the true audience effect neither of the two types of facilitation cited by Allport are obviously at work,—neither rivalry nor the contributory stimuli afforded by the work of others. The study of the co-working group is thus only a transition stage toward the study of the effect of the audience alone, on which topic fewer investigations are available.

"Working in the presence of others," writes Allport, "even though there is no direct contact nor communication, establishes certain fundamental attitudes. We are confused and distracted whenever we feel our reaction to be at variance with or inferior to the average behavior of those about us. In the association process we tend to inhibit egocentric trends and personal complexes. In our thinking we assume a conversational attitude, becoming more expansive and less precise. And finally, we avoid extremes in passing judgment, tending, often unconsciously, toward conformity with what we think to be the opinion of those about us."

EXPERIMENTS BEFORE AUDIENCES

H. T. Moore [48] has reported an experiment in which the influence of various distracting situations was determined by showing their interference with work in mental multiplication. Twenty men subjects were used. One of the distractions employed was the embarrassment occasioned by being required to carry on mental work before an audience.

"In order to test the degree to which the subject's mental operations would be retarded by his having to face a crowd, he was given four problems to solve while seated conspicuously in the presence of a classroom full of watching students. In most cases the number of on-lookers was 65, but for a few men it was necessary to use a group of 23."

The amount of distraction caused by the complete array of situations, supposedly arousing fear, anger, sex interest, and embarrassment by an audience was computed, by comparing records made under these circumstances with the normal undistracted performance. This distraction average was then used as a base, and the influence of the special factors determined by comparing their effects with the general distraction average.

In the case of embarrassment by the audience nine of the men showed more than average distraction, and eleven showed less than the general distraction average. The average result for the twenty subjects was actually 3.5 per cent less than the general distraction average. Individual differences were very considerable, and there was no close correlation between effect in this situation and effect in the case of the other induced emotional states. Fear and anger, produced in a variety of ways, showed influences of much greater magnitude, and in the direction of positive distraction.

Moore's data, as published, do not allow us to conclude that the audience had actually no distracting nor stimulating effect upon the mental work attempted, since he does not give data that show the "normal," or undistracted standards. Moreover, the variability of the records is great, and no allowance is made for the possible effects of practice, which are likely to be great in the case of mental multiplication. The data show merely that the effect of the audience, by way of distraction, is less than that caused by the fear and anger stimuli used by the investigator, but somewhat greater than the distraction caused by the stimuli to sex interest and repulsion. The latter two situations, indeed, showed average improvements of 10 per cent and 16 per cent above the general distraction average. The most striking result is in the great variability of the data for the different men. The effects of the audience, so far as these data indicate them, range all the way from a stimulating effect of 148 per cent to a distracting effect of 60 per cent, as compared with the general distraction average.

EXPERIMENTS OF GATES, TRAVIS, AND BURTT

G. S. Gates [20] has experimentally investigated the influence of the mere presence of a small audience (half a dozen spectators) and a larger audience (thirty to forty spectators) on the ability of college women to perform in such relatively simple standard tests as co-ordination, color naming, giving analogies, and word naming. In all sixty-two subjects were studied, by a carefully controlled technique which was so planned as to eliminate various sources of error and so as to make comparison reliable. All the "audience" subjects did the tests alone (except for the examiner) and also before one or other of the audiences. The measure of influence of the changed conditions is the change in performance, when this is compared with the change in the case of a control group who twice performed the tests alone.

Under these conditions, with an inactive audience, with these sophisticated subjects and the relatively simple work processes, the measurable influence of the audience is found to be slight. In the case of "the most difficult test, that of naming words . . . there is a slight possibility of the existence of a stimulating effect due to a large audience. . . . If it is possible to use as evidence the direction of slight differences, we might argue from their consistency, which is evident when we consider either the amount of improvement or the percentage of subjects improving," that in general the influence of the audience was detrimental. Also, "There is a suggestion that the better individuals in three tests are disturbed more than are the medium and poor subjects by the presence of spectators."

This investigation deliberately studied the effect of the mere presence of spectators, excluding any expression, on the part of the audience, of antagonism or enthusiasm. The absence of striking results may be due to one or more of a variety of causes, and it is interesting to contrast these small influences with the marked subjective changes that come to the performer when appearing before an audience. Thus it may be that these subjects were so well adapted to the presence of their college associates that their observation had no influence of a marked degree. Or the mental processes measured may have been of too simple an order to show such influences as might have been observed in more complicated performances. Or individuals might have been differently affected, some disturbed, some stimulated, so that in this case the averaging of results would cancel out the true picture. Or finally, it may be that it is not so much the mere presence of an audience, but in the main their attitude, as of encouragement and sympathy or apathy and antagonism, or perhaps merely the uncertainty of what the attitude will be, that is influential in the usual case. For some evidence that the attitude of the audience has a measurable influence on performance, we may turn to other experiments.

Results very similar to those reported by Gates were secured in an experiment by Travis [64] on the effect of a small audience upon visual-manual co-ordination. The task used was that of holding a flexible pointer on a revolving target. Twenty-two subjects, all but two being college freshmen (boys), were given preliminary training in the performance, so as to bring them to a practice level. They were then given a number of trials before small audiences.

The audiences contained four to eight people, both men and women, chosen from the student body. The members of the audience were not acquainted with the performers. The attitude of the audience was passive, that is, although strict attention was given to the work of the performer, no comments were made, and no indication of approval or disapproval.

Only four of the twenty-two subjects failed to give better performances before their audiences than they had been able to give on their best occasions when working without spectators. The investigator shows however that the actual differences were very small, the average superiority being only about two and one-half times as large as the probable error. Of course it should be observed that when performers have reached an approximate practice level of achievement, only very small changes can be expected in the direction of superiority.

Travis concludes that "there is an indication of superior eye-hand co-ordination among the subjects tested in the social situation. Statistically considered the degree of superiority is not sufficient to be very reliable. Yet a study of individual performances leaves no doubt as to the fact that the influence of the audience materially raises the score."

An experiment by Burtt [11] shows that the performer

may experience significant internal changes in the presence of the audience, even though no obvious external modifications of conduct are present. Burtt's subjects were in some cases to tell the truth about situations of which they had been informed. In other cases they were to give false reports about these situations, meanwhile attempting to conceal from the observers the fact of their deception. The problem was thus to arouse the consciousness of deception and to compare this condition with that involved in the consciousness of telling the truth.

Changes in breathing rate and in blood pressure have been found present during the telling of falsehoods. Burtt recorded the breathing rate and the blood pressure changes of these subjects, both when lying and when telling the truth, and both without an audience and on occasions when "a number of persons—from 3 to 26— were present watching the subject and trying to determine his guilt or innocence from his reactions."

Without an audience, the breathing ratios failed to differentiate "Lie" from "Truth." The blood pressure records correctly differentiated in 71 per cent of the cases. Before the audience, however, the breathing ratios diagnosed the lie or truth correctly in 73 per cent of the cases and in 91 per cent of the cases the blood pressure changes did so. Evidently the presence of the audience enhanced the internal bodily changes and the correlated emotional experiences.

It is of special interest also that, although the instrumental measurements of these delicate changes afforded such a preponderance of correct diagnoses, the judgments of the members of the audience, based on directly observable behavior, were entirely untrustworthy. They showed only chance agreement with the facts.

The situation here is much like that found in the case of other disturbing agents, such as distractions, fatigue, and drugs. The internal changes, introspectively or instrumentally observed, are more informative than are judgments based on general conduct or overt behavior. In general it seems to be true that the obvious changes in performance, due to the influence of the audience, are smaller than the performer, on the basis of his self observation, supposes them to be.

Nearly every one is well acquainted with the general nature of the subjective experiences constituting stage fright. The following, from one collection of reports on these experiences [23] are typical:

A finds himself wishing he were not a man, so that he could wear skirts to hide his knees which shake so together that he is sure every one notices them.

B never worries over the excellence of his performance, but is constantly fearful lest he commit some irrelevant bit of awkwardness, such as losing his garter or falling off the platform.

C finds it impossible to utter any words at all. The worst thing about it is the violent heart beat which makes it impossible to speak even very simple things.

D finds that the audience appears as one vague blur, in which the individual members cannot be distinguished. When they are seen they look like cats, grinning in derision.

E is a violinist. His hands perspire so that he cannot maintain a tone on the instrument; his left hand grows cold; the bow arm becomes stiff and heavy and seems to do awkward things of its own accord rather than the intended movements.

F suffers from nausea and a stomach upset that results in illness that puts her to bed for several days.

THE ATTITUDE OF THE AUDIENCE

It seems obvious that not all of the effect of an audience comes from the mere presence of spectators. Their attitude toward the actor has a very real influence as well. But few experimental data are available on this factor, and even these are usually for the influence of one or two spectators, and their attitude, rather than for the effect of larger groups. In general, the attitude of an audience may be characterized as favorable or encouraging, unfavorable or discouraging, and indifferent or neutral. Perhaps indifference belongs psychologically with discouragement.

Gilchrist [22] has reported results showing an astounding effect of encouragement and discouragement by a spectator's comments, on the test performance of college students. Two groups were given independently, a certain mental test. In the case of one group (29 subjects) the experimenter then said—"A hasty examination of the papers in the test just given shows that the members of this group did *exceptionally well*. I ask you to take the test again." In the case of the other group (21 subjects) the experimenter said, "A hasty examination of the papers in the tests just given shows that the members of this group *did not do so well in the test as the average 12-year old child would do*. I ask you to take the test again." The encouraged group improved 79 per cent in the second test; the discouraged group deteriorated 6 per cent in the second test. The great difference is attributed to the praise and reproof. Perhaps these results are complicated by other motives, indirectly aroused by the comments offered.

Gates and Rissland [21] worked with 74 subjects (college students) and two tests individually given. There were three groups of subjects, and each person did each of the two tests twice. After the first trial the members of one group were told "That is really splendid! Do you always make such good scores? In a curve of distribution your score would be away up here (indicating a position at the top of the curve). Your score was so good that I wonder if you would mind repeating the test."

Members of the second group, after the first trials, were told, "Oh dear, that is really a very poor score. I am afraid that you would fall at the bottom of the curve of distribution. I wonder if you would mind repeating the test." Members of the third group were given two trials at each test, without any comment. This gives then an *encouraged*, a *discouraged*, and a *control* group, the motivation consisting in the attitude and expressed opinion of the spectator or auditor.

The results are by no means so striking as those reported by Gilchrist. The experimenters conclude,—"We might say then (with the usual realization of the inadequacy of the data), that it is better to make some comment about the score than to make none; that it is better to make an encouraging than a discouraging remark; that relatively poor individuals are more likely to be unfavorably affected by discouragement than are relatively proficient persons; that the effect of these incentives does not seem to be constant for the two tests."

The following table shows the per cent of improvement, and the percentage of subjects improving, in the two tests, and the three groups.

| | CO-ORDINATION | | COLOR NAMING | |
INCENTIVE	Average Improvement, Taps per Minute	Number of Subjects Improving	Average Improvement, Seconds	Number of Subjects Improving
Encouragement .	8.7	89%	0.4	58%
Discouragement .	5.4	70	0.7	51
Repetition only .	4.9	64	−1.4	44

The variability of the individual scores is so great as to make the quantitative comparisons very unreliable, however, as the authors carefully point out.

THE EFFECT OF "RAZZING"

Just as Gates studied the effect of the mere presence of an audience, with the attitude constant, so Laird [39] has studied the influence of the attitude of the audience. Rate of tapping, three-hole co-ordination, and steadiness, both standing and sitting, were the tests employed. In the one instance college boys, as part of a fraternity initiation, made the best records they could in these tests, with an audience of their fellows present but maintaining an attitude of respectful silence. On the other occasion the same boys were required to perform the same tests before a group of their fellows, the auditors meanwhile making every possible effort to discourage the performer by their free remarks and general attitude.

In all the subjects, steadiness was diminished before the hostile audience. Co-ordination skill also decreased, but not so markedly nor so uniformly as steadiness. Tapping rate showed no loss, five of the subjects, on the other hand showing better scores. Actually these results are clouded by the probable practice effect present in the second ("razzing") trial, and since the experimenter made no control tests of the effect of mere repetition, the main conclusion must be that the effects of a discouraging audience are probably even more disastrous than these data suggest.

That greater effort was induced by the "razzing" is shown by the accounts of violent performance under those conditions, to the extent of breaking the tapping stylus and one of the co-ordination counters in this part of the experiment.

Striking individual differences in susceptibility to the hostility of the audience are noted, and the investigator remarks that "Some stars of the diamond are so affected by the rooters' cheers and catcalls that they are put into the game principally when on a friendly field. Others seem to be benefited by the discouraging element among the rooters."

THE ABSENT AUDIENCE

We have already had occasion to refer to that use of the word "audience" which relates it to the writer, the architect, the composer. The influence here is remote, inasmuch as the audience is neither in time nor in space confronting the performer, and is at the most a purely hypothetical number of individuals, who may, as auditors or spectators, never be congregated.

But there is, in our own time, an intermediate type of audience, which although absent in space and showing none of the phenomena of congregation, are nevertheless actual auditors at the time of the performance. This is the case in radio broadcasting, and many performers report entirely new experiences from speaking or singing into the receiver, with the knowledge that all over the country there are at that moment auditors who are listening to the performance, either alone or in small groups. The mere thought of this distant audience, present in time but absent in space, seems to have effects on the performer not unlike those exerted by the perceptual presence of an audience. Individual differences also appear in these reactions.

Thus one famous and experienced singer is reported to have said, after his first broadcasting experience:

"I like it. You know I've had plenty of experience making records, but this beats it. Somehow you seem to be able to visualize an audience better in broadcasting and you can sing to them directly. After you get the hang of it, it's easy."

Another famous opera singer, broadcasting for the first time and reporting her experience, is said to have "confessed that she was badly frightened at the beginning." The interview further reports her as remarking:

"Oh, I just thought of those 6,000,000 people out somewhere listening to me, and I was scared to death. I generally sing to four or five thousand, and it's very different. It's odd what a feeling you get, when you see that little instrument in front of you. I had to fight to keep myself from tightening all up, but after I got well started I forgot it."

Nothing is known, through exact experiment, concerning these effects of the absent audience, and the ways in which they resemble and differ from those of the perceptually present congregation,—whether the differences are of kind or only of degree, whether individual differences are common to the two situations. Such studies offer interesting possibilities, inasmuch as we are here concerned not only with the effects of an audience, but also with the nature of a thought as distinguished from an immediate perception.

It is clear from these accounts that experimentation in this field has only made a beginning. The analysis of individual differences, the extension of the types of performance into the more complicated field of higher mental activity and more complicated motor activity, and numerous related topics, afford inviting problems for future investigations of the influence of the audience upon the performer.

SUMMARY OF EXPERIMENTAL RESULTS

This survey of such experiments as have already been undertaken in this field yields conclusions that are only tentative, at best.   The following suggestions seem to be more or less clearly indicated, however.

1. Working in the presence of others (co-workers) results in a greater output of work, especially if this work involves muscular performance.   But the original-ity and the quality of such work suffer if the work should involve careful discrimination, judgment, and thought-fulness.

2. This stimulation by fellow-workers seems to depend on two general influences: (*a*) the new incentives af-forded by rivalry and competition; and (*b*) the dyna-mogenic effects and the suggestive stimulation provided by the work-sounds, which become associated with the act of performance and are magnified when many work together.

3. The influence of the passive audience seems to be small, in the case of such relatively simple types of per-formance as have been studied.   The effect seems to be chiefly on the worker's feelings rather than on his actual efficiency of performance.

4. Different types of performance do not all follow the same law, under the influence of the passive audience. In general the effect is similar to that of the presence of fellow-workers.   Motor dexterities are stimulated, and the quantity of work tends to increase, except when it involves logical accuracy and intellectual precision.

5. Individual differences among performers, in these effects, are very marked, often being opposite in char-acter.   The basis of these individual differences has not yet been adequately explored.

6. The most striking results are those secured when the audience actively registers its approval or disapproval of the performance.   This suggests that it is the attitude of the audience, rather than its mere presence that is the effective factor in such results as have been experimentally demonstrated.

PRACTICAL CONCLUSIONS

1. Without an audience women relapse and men become unkempt.

2. The effects of an audience on the performer seem less obvious in his overt performance than they appear in his subjective experience; stage fright usually feels more disturbing than it appears to the audience.

3. The presence of the audience and its attitude are two different facts; it is the latter that most readily produces measurable effects on the performer.

4. Stimulation of performance by an audience is likely to increase its rate and vigor at the expense of its quality in other respects.

5. The most striking fact about the influence of the audience is its great variability in the case of different performers.

CHAPTER XIII

THE PSYCHOLOGY OF STAGE FRIGHT

TYPES OF ATTENTION AND ATTITUDE

Further investigation of these problems may to advantage take their start from observations concerning the attitudes taken by different people in facing other types of difficulty. Thus in Ruger's study [59] of the solving of mechanical puzzles, he found indications of three distinguishable "attitudes" or "directions of attention." In the first place was the "problem attitude," in which the worker paid no special attention to the observer nor to himself, but devoted his attention exclusively to the problem, the puzzle before him, as a task to be handled. This was the most favorable attitude for problem solution. But two other attitudes or directions of attention were also sometimes observed, both of which interfered with efficient puzzle solution.

One of these interfering attitudes Ruger called the "self-attentive." In this attitude "attention is not on the problem but on the self." The self is felt to be on trial. "What sort of a self shall I and others consider myself to be?" is the question which occupies attention, and this is usually accompanied by a state of worry, of emotional tension, which still further distracts from the problem in hand.

The effects of the "self-attentive" attitude upon processes which might otherwise run an automatic course is neatly illustrated by the familiar verse celebrating the fate of the centipede, in a similar circumstance.

> "A centipede was happy quite
> Until a frog in fun
> Said 'Pray, which leg comes after which?'
> This raised her mind to such a pitch,
> She lay distracted in a ditch,
> Considering how to run."

The other interfering attitude is the "suggestible" one. This "appears in the presence of a person supposed to 'know the answer.' The object of attention is here the person with the prestige suggestion, rather than the problem itself. . . . In the puzzle experiments this tendency was so marked with two of the subjects that it was necessary for the operator to screen himself entirely from view in order that slight movements of his should not be taken, correctly or erroneously, as indications of the correctness or incorrectness of certain manipulations."

It is also interesting to note that "the occurrence of these (interfering) attitudes was especially prominent in the first attempts of a subject with his first puzzle. In some cases the first success brought a complete reversal of attitude in dealing with later puzzles."

In the giving of psychological examinations to individuals, which is also a social situation inasmuch as the examiner confronts the candidate and presents him with a series of questions or tasks, these three attitudes are very obvious. One child, for example, is so conscious that he is being tested, graded, evaluated, that his whole attention is given to the impression he is presumably making. His replies are more or less stilted or artificial, his flow of expression is inhibited, or there may be an exaggeration of facial expression, meticulous choice of words, and a fearful approach that clearly interferes with the exhibition of his best talents.

Another child is intent upon the examiner, observing his every reaction, facial expression, and gesture. He asks after each of his own replies, "Is that right?" and is clearly looking for clues and suggestions as to just what type of answer would most please the examiner. This attitude also gives an artificial expression of the candidate's spontaneous tendencies and abilities.

A third child takes definitely the problem attitude. Ignoring his own mannerisms, clothing, and posture, and paying scant attention to the expressive indications of approval or disapproval, he attacks the questions or task definitely as a problem to be solved, and devotes to its solution his undivided attention. This is easily the most favorable attitude for the exhibition of the candidate's native talents, and is encouraged by all skillful mental examiners.

It seems likely that performers before a typical audience assume one of these characteristics, or some combination of them, and that the attitude taken is closely related to the freedom and confidence of the performance, and therefore to the emotional state of the performer. Moreover, as in the case of the puzzle experiments, in the first appearances before audiences these interfering attitudes may be most conspicuous. If these appearances meet with success, the attitude may be reversed, tending more exclusively toward the problem type,—with absorption in the subject matter rather than in the auditors or in the performer's own self. Improvement comes from dropping the unfavorable attitudes in favor of the more efficient one, and results from a combination of native tendency, initial success, and adaptation through repetition.

Future studies may well take account of these attitudes in connection with the effects of appearance before an audience. It may even be found that the most favorable type of attitude or combination of attitudes varies somewhat with the nature of the occasion and the motive of the performer.

Finally we may raise the question as to the precise nature of the emotional effects experienced before the audience. It is not obvious, at first glance, for example, whether the effects are those of embarrassment, of excitement, of self-consciousness, of humiliation and submission, of timidity and fear, or of distraction.

BASHFULNESS AND STAGE FRIGHT

Some discussions of bashfulness and embarrassment may be confused with the consideration of stage fright. And it may be that what some report as mild degrees of this condition are only bashfulness, such as children are likely to show after the age of about three years. We may therefore profitably consider first the analysis of this mental experience, as given by McDougall.[43] He declares that there is no element of fear in it. Instead, it is "symptomatic of a struggle between two opposed impulses of the instincts of self-display and self-abasement," within the self-regarding sentiment.

"The slightly painful agitation that most of us feel when we have to figure before an audience seems to me to be of the same nature as this childish bashfulness. . . . Our negative self-feeling is evoked by the presence of persons whom we regard as our superiors, or who, by reason of their number and of their forming a collective whole, are able to make on us an impression of power, but it is not until our positive self-feeling is also excited, until we feel ourselves called upon to make a display of ourselves or our powers, to address the audience, to play a part as an equal among the superior beings, or even merely to walk across the room before the eyes of a crowd, that we experience the slightly painful, slightly pleasurable, but often very intense emotional agitation which is properly called bashfulness."

But the stage fright we are considering here is not· mere bashfulness. It may in some cases, in which shame is the principal element, be closely related to bashfulness, and due, as McDougall suggests, to conflict between "the twin impulses of the self-regarding sentiment." But trembling, palpitation, perspiration, dryness of the mucous membranes, secretory and excretory disturbances, paralysis, and similar complaints of the stage-shocked subject are tokens of something very different from bashfulness. They are, for example, far from being "slightly pleasurable," although they may perhaps be called exciting. We must suppose therefore that the account of. bashfulness is· not entirely adequate to the explanation of stage fright.

It is however instructive to consider the type of explanation here offered for bashfulness, for since conflict between two impulses may result in such a conspicuous experience as embarrassment, in its various degrees, it is conceivable that the general notion of conflict, but between perhaps more vigorous impulses, may be applicable to stage fright also.

THEORETICAL ANALYSIS

Popular terminology at least suggests that the reaction to an audience, when this takes the form of interference with freedom of conduct, is a form of fear reaction,—a reaction to danger. "Stage fright" is the term in common use. If stage fright is really related to other forms of fear and is in fact a reaction to danger, we may ask just what its relation is to the other varieties of fear reaction.

In a detailed discussion of the fear instinct Rivers [57] points out that "five chief forms of reaction to danger can be distinguished, other forms seeming to be modifications or combinations of these."

A—*Flight*. Associated with flight as a reaction is the emotion of fear, which is expecially pronounced when flight is interfered with and which may perhaps also accompany normal and unimpeded flight.

B—*Aggression*. The opposite of flight, comes into play only when the source of danger is another animal, is accompanied by the emotion of anger, and is a later form of reaction, genetically, than that of flight.

C—*Immobility*. This inhibition of movement, suppression of activity, is one of the most primitive modes of response, found even on a barely physiological plane. Its value lies in the concealment afforded. The state accompanying this reaction is that of unconsciousness through suppression of fear and pain.

D—*Collapse*. This is characterized by tremors or irregular movements and represents actually a breakdown of the instinctive reactions provided for danger situations. It is especially characteristic of man and the higher animals, and is accompanied by that excessive emotion which we call terror. It is displayed especially when an instinctive tendency is frustrated, and represents a state of conflict.

E—*Manipulative Activity*. With no affective accompaniment. This is the type of reaction characterized by "directly serviceable acts"—such as handling weapons, manipulating the wheel, applying the brakes, sounding an alarm, etc. It is "the normal reaction of the healthy man."

Rivers then attempts to relate the various neuroses to the exaggeration and fixation of these various modes of danger response. It is clear that "stage fright" represents neither A, B, C, nor E. It is apparently most clearly the D type, the collapse reaction. But perhaps tendencies toward these various reactions may be enough to afford a descriptive classification of audience effects in something like the following manner.

A. Flight leads merely to avoidance of the situation of facing an audience, and is a common reaction.

B. Aggression represents the reaction of the individual who is "stimulated" by an audience or by spectators.

C. Immobility represents the paralysis, the loss of memory, the aphasia, and the inability to proceed because of a blank and empty consciousness, often shown by children who "forget their part."

D. Collapse represents the premonitory symptoms, felt before the audience is faced, or while sitting in the speaker's chair, or perhaps continued throughout the appearance.

E. Manipulative activity would represent the absence of emotional state and is the condition which the ordinary speaker longs to make his own.

The characteristic reactions of speakers before audiences seem thus to fall in line well enough with the descriptions of the danger reactions, and this at least suggests that "stage fright" represents a definite instinctive adjustment to a danger signal, the danger then being the assembled crowd. And there is indeed plenty of reason for supposing that a "crowd" could become the appropriate stimulus for an instinctive danger reaction, as easily as a noise, a shock, or a sudden pain, a large object, a suddenly moving object, etc. But as suggested at another point, this naming of the reaction to an audience is not an explanation of it, but merely a classification.

Or may we say that the two tendencies, to crave an audience and to fear a crowd, both represent opposed instinctive urges, and that the particular reaction to an audience will depend on the relations of conflict on the one hand or reinforcement on the other, of these two trends? If so, stage fright would represent a neurosis, at least according to Rivers' account of the nature of a neurosis.

A NEUROSIS THEORY—CONFLICT

There seems to be abundant evidence that, even in the lower animals, a stress neurosis may arise on the basis of two conflicting tendencies, of approximately equal strength. A robin who has built its nest under the porch roof of a summer cottage may display just such a picture of distress when the summer resident appears and occupies the porch chair. First the bird flies toward the nest in the already accustomed way. At once it encounters the new and fearful object, and whirls about, retreating to a given distance, with both objects, the nest and the human being, in the general line of view.

It alights on a branch and hops about frantically, uttering varied sounds of discontent and fright. In time it flies across to a branch from which the dreaded object cannot be seen, then suddenly darts forth for the nest again, only to be abruptly checked when the human figure again comes in view. Caught in this vicious circle it may repeatedly traverse the ineffectual path, becoming meanwhile more and more wrought up, vocal and agitated. It is a typical picture of emotional neurosis, occasioned by the conflict of two strong tendencies, one leading toward and the other away from the vicinity of the nest.

If we were strongly inclined toward the instinct doctrine of human behavior, we might suppose that the two different instincts were common to the human species. The one would be described as the fear of the strange pack or crowd. We might show on evolutionary grounds how serviceable such an instinct would have been in primitive times, leading to a general wariness of strange groups of other human beings, and to personal safety through flight. Such a vestigial instinct might be supposed to persist in modern life, although its original justification would have largely disappeared.

On the other hand we might suppose something like an instinct for exhibitionism or self display, which would be the basis for the "craving for an audience" which we have already described. Primitively one of these instincts might have been so much stronger than the other that prolonged conflict seldom ensued. But in modern life the encounter of strange groups is so common an experience that we may suppose the "flight" instinct to have become weakened through adaptation, or perhaps to be gradually becoming weaker since natural selection would no longer operate to perpetuate it.

If two such original tendencies should be of approximately equal strength, we might suppose that they would, in modern life, be frequently brought into sustained conflict. Such a condition would produce an emotional neurosis, resembling the agitation of the robin. Thus we might explain the occurrence of stage fright, which might either become fixed as a habit, or lost through adaptation. Even the robin's conflict was in time solved as the strange object became more and more familiar. The bird, in its successive flights, approached nearer and nearer, finally sailing triumphantly past the stranger in the chair, and setting comfortably upon its nest.

STAGE FRIGHT AS A LEARNED REACTION

The explanation in terms of "instincts," however, presents many difficulties, and the concept of instinct is much less used in psychology than was formerly the case. In addition, the most recent observations of the common complaint known as stage fright suggest that the condition has an individual rather than a racial origin. A number of cases of stage fright have been studied and treated by Goodhue,[23] who is convinced that such a condition always dates back to some earlier experience— "a first cause—the splinter that causes the pain." This earlier episode or experience may not be remembered by the sufferer, but often it can be discovered by a little questioning, and when thus recalled often arouses amazement.

Certainly Goodhue is able to quote plenty of cases which appear to fit in with this interpretation. Thus one young woman always suffered from extreme nervousness when appearing on a public platform; she was also observed to be particularly fastidious about her clothing on such occasions. Investigation succeeded in tracing the nervousness back to her high school days. Ordinarily she had suffered no nervousness; but on one occasion, on stepping to the platform, she was dismayed to see in a mirror on the wall that her slip had dropped down below her skirt. She struggled to correct this disarrangement, became panicky, and finally fled from the stage with a gesture of helplessness. Her adult addiction to stage fright seemed to be due to this early embarrassment. According to Goodhue:

"Her personal appearance had no connection with the quality of her work as a speaker, and if she had not happened to have seen the under-slip she would have acquitted herself with credit. But having been shocked by this trifling incident she always joined the impression of inferiority and shame with the fact that she was facing an audience."

Supported by such instances as this, Goodhue develops the following account and explanation of the origin of stage fright.

"Stage fright is the association of fear with inferiority, rising insidiously to the surface and expressing itself in great mental and bodily suffering."

"The first cause may have been trivial and apparently not connected with a public appearance. Because it has passed unnoticed, the lack of observation became its deadliest factor. Nevertheless it was always *something* or *some one* that caused the feeling of fear."

"Even if not connected with the act of public appearance, this inferiority-cause associates itself within a short time *with* a public appearance. As a result, every time the artist approaches the platform he carries with him his feelings which include those of inferiority. With each repetition and its attendant misunderstanding, the inferiority becomes more pronounced."

Such an explanation is at least consonant with the usual behavior of emotional experience.[27] Emotions characteristically may be reinstated, once they have occurred, by slight and partial features of the total situation in which they were originally provoked. In the case just described, the partial detail, "being before an audience," is supposed to have been effective in arousing just such shame and inhibition as formerly followed upon the much more complex situation of her high school embarrassment. We might well expect that not only shame and embarrassment, but fear also might thus be reinstated by details not originally responsible for them. The following case appears to illustrate such a condition.

A singer of long and successful experience was unable to account for severe stage fright that had recently overcome her and filled her with panic. No episode involving inferiority was discovered through questioning, but a recent fright was found to have occurred on an occasion in which "a crowd of people" was an important part of the total situation.

While riding in a crowded street car, a short circuit caused a sudden flash and filled the air with smoke. The singer was crushed by the clamoring crowd trying to get out of the car. All were in terror. Rushing toward the door she found it locked. For some time this distressing jam continued until finally the door was opened and the terror-stricken occupants of the car released. The singer reported that for a while she felt she was being choked to death by the acrid fumes of the smoke, and that she was just on the point of falling into unconsciousness when relief came.

Thereafter any crowded hall, a packed audience, or an overheated building brought back to her a "terror of suffocation." She had to retire in a panic and her career threatened to be definitely and seriously interfered with. Here again slight details or partial features of the earlier terror scene tend to bring on a somewhat milder panic, but one of the same kind as that experienced on the original occasion. Such a slight detail is what we call a sign or cue; it is, in other words, a symbol, a thought. That thoughts may be as powerful as things is a commonplace. Every doctor takes advantage of this principle when he prescribes a bread-pill, a colored water, or other "placebo."

Goodhue also describes another case in which a music student was filled with "mortification and disgrace" by a scathing letter received from her violin teacher, an appointment with whom she had failed to keep. Apologies were duly presented, but in spite of this, at the concert for which this teacher had been preparing her "when she started to play the terror of inferiority swept over her like a flood, and its tide arose again and again every time she appeared in later concerts." Here again, an embarrassment originating in a social situation quite remote from an audience appeared as stage fright; but the feeling was not primarily due to the audience, nor to the stage; it was due to subtle details of the concert playing situation, for these were also essential features of the original dismay over the letter of her concert teacher.

To the question,—"What is the cause of stage fright?" the answer may vary with the person concerned. We have considered three different types of explanation that have been offered. Perhaps the effect of an audience differs with the performer, so that sometimes one type of explanation and sometimes another is applicable. In most cases it is likely that more than one factor is responsible, or that some combination of these different explanations may be required. All three theories fit reasonably well the phenomena of stage fright; reasonably good psychological warrant attaches to all the theories, and one is about as feasible as another. The three explanations may be briefly summarized as follows:

1. Stage fright may be a direct fear phenomenon, in which serviceable manipulation gives way to flight, tremor, paralysis, collapse, or aggressiveness.

2. Or stage fright may be an emotional neurosis, occasioned by the conflict of two competing tendencies or instincts, of approximately equal strength.

3. Or stage fright may be a simple emotional redintegration, in which some disabling emotion is reinstated by the presence of some feature of the more complex situation in which the emotion originally arose,—whether the emotion be that of shame, inferiority feeling, or fright.

THE CURE OF STAGE FRIGHT

Goodhue [23] reports that methods of treatment used by her brought distinct relief to those undergoing them. Part of the treatment consists of various "exercises," designed to promote confidence, relaxation, and poise, and to suggest success rather than failure. This is a constructive method of building up opposed attitudes.

But Goodhue believes that the thorough cure of stage fright is achieved only when its origin is discovered in the individual's past life. Much importance is then attached to "uncovering the complex," that is, revealing the early shock, a distressing experience now probably gone from the sufferer's ready recollection. This psychoanalysis thus stands out as the essential feature of a complete treatment and cure.

It is probable that this feature of the cure has been overemphasized. The statement that discovery of the initial complex cures the trouble is far too simple. In the case of other neuroses much more than this is really required, although the process of "discovering the complex" may be the most obvious feature, and perhaps the only feature of which the patient is aware.

For all common neuroses an actual re-education is required as part of any effective therapy. The "discovery of the complex" serves only to suggest the direction which this re-education may profitably take. The endeavor to discover the alleged complex commonly leads to prolonged conversation about the situation that is finally blamed for the trouble, to a reconsideration of the importance of the elements involved in it, to reflective adjustment on an intelligent level, instead of the direct emotional attitude formerly taken.

The new estimate thus given to the earlier experience as now remembered and reviewed may result in new situations of that kind being faced with a different attitude. The elements responsible for the old dread may even come to arouse amusement or some other emotion quite different from fright or shame or inferiority feeling.

"Suppose a child is frightened unduly by the sound of objects falling upon the roof of its bed chamber. It may easily be discovered that such fright dates from earlier experiences in which objects were thrown at one by angry playmates, or from tales of bombardment, of terrible falling stars, and the like. But the mere discovery of this origin does not relieve the child's fear. The fears are easily allayed however by explaining verbally, or concretely demonstrating, that the noises are produced by acorns falling from the oak tree which stands alongside the house. The perceptual character of the stimulus is thus changed, through a process of re-education, through new and reflective insight concerning the fearful object. Discovery of the origin of the fear served only to show that it was an acquired reaction, in terms of past experiences, not an instinctive fright reaction. It thus served to indicate the feasibility of cure and the probable direction of the most promising therapy." [27]

Experiments have been made with the fears of children and various techniques of cure tried out in a comparative way. Among the techniques thus attempted were such things as social disapproval, verbal discussion, imitation of fearless ones, adaptation through persistent encountering of the dreaded object, shame and ridicule, and "reconditioning." By the reconditioning is meant simply the deliberate attachment of more desirable effects to the stimulus. Thus the child who fears the rain may be allowed to wear its beloved red cap and coat only when going out into the rain. Rainy days thus acquire a "new meaning," a joyful one. In time, and with frequent experience, the rain itself may come to be delighted in, quite as inexplicably as it was formerly feared. The fear has been cured by its replacement. The emotion has not been roughly suppressed or inhibited. Another emotion has been substituted for it in connection with the once dreaded object.

If stage fright is a direct fear experience, perhaps instinctive in origin, that therapy is most hopeful which proceeds by giving emphasis to some different emotion, through vividness and repetition. Confidence and enthusiasm must be connected with the appearance of an audience, through experience.

If stage fright is instead a conflict neurosis, due to two competing tendencies, one of which is fear, such conflict can be eliminated therapeutically by strengthening the rival emotion through deliberate exercise and planned experience.

If stage fright is a simple emotional redintegration, the effective treatment will consist in discovering its stimulus and attaching to this stimulus new outcomes and consequences. If stage fright is some combination of these three effects, since all require the same mode of therapy, the procedure will be identical. On any of the three theories of stage fright the same mode of treatment is required. This is the substitution of some other emotion in the place of fright through re-education.

The good results coming from the treatment described by Goodhue would appear therefore to result more from the exercises in "confidence and poise" than from the "discovery of the complex." Such exercises may constitute a re-education, and their value may be further enhanced by an emphasis on this aspect of their affectiveness.

Such considerations as the following suggest the nature of the general principles to be followed. There is more than one stimulus involved when the frightened violin player, for example, confronts his audience. The presence of the audience is a stimulus. Holding and playing the instrument is another. If both these have been part of the original fear situation, their joint effect will be greater than that exercised by either alone.

Handling and playing the instrument, away from audiences, might now be made to yield confidence and pleasure, by circumstances so arranged that this act would give such feelings. Or less formidable audiences might first be confronted, such as audiences of children. On the other hand the presence of an audience as a stimulus should also be independently treated. Audiences should be faced successfully in other acts than handling the violin. Amateur dramatics, public speaking, or teaching small groups might thus be made to give confidence in such a connection.

In this way both stimuli might be "trained" independently, each in contexts giving a feeling of success. Only after this is achieved should the two then be combined; and at first even this should be done before audiences known to be favorably disposed, or friendly, or young or otherwise encouraging.

In any other case where several features can be identified in the cause of stage fright, this method of adapting separately to the different features and then to their combination would appear to be indicated. Other methods often resolve themselves into this, as when adaptation comes through repeated trial which permits success to supervene upon failure.

THE AUDIENCE AND THE DRUG EFFECT

There is a certain analogy between the effect of the audience and the effect of distraction, obstacles, and dangers. Experiments on distraction have usually resulted in the rather paradoxical finding that the distractions employed produced better rather than inferior work.

Morgan,[51] likewise, has shown very clearly than an individual's "greatest strength" can be increased by setting him to work against a greater mechanical resistance. Such results show that when we are working "at our best," this usually means merely the best that the circumstances provoke. Introduce obstacle, distraction, a rival, witness, or audience, and the improvement in accomplishment shows that reserve energy and skill were available that were not called out by the simpler circumstances. Increased zeal results in greater power. The obstacle, distraction, rival, witness, and audience are dynamogenic in their effect.

Now it is a general rule that increased effort and conscious striving are not similarly effective throughout their whole range. Up to a certain point effort and attention facilitate performance. Beyond that point they result in interference, unsteadiness, inco-ordination and self-consciousness. Thereupon work may proceed less smoothly, more erratically and perhaps more slowly. Such agents seem to function in the same fashion as does a drug like caffein. The results vary with the amount of the dose, with the type of work that is involved, and with the individual concerned.[28]

If only motor speed is involved, this drug produces more rapid work, and the gain in speed varies directly with the size of the dose, within experimental limits. But if steadiness is involved, even minute doses produce impairment. If accurate co-ordination and discriminative judgment are involved, small doses are stimulating and produce superior work. But doses beyond a certain amount produce an overstimulation, which is damaging to accuracy and subversive of judgment. The impetuous nervous system outruns itself and poorer rather than improved work is the result of excessive stimulation.

The audience apparently functions in a similar way. Small doses stimulate; they satisfy the craving for an audience. But beyond the optimum amount the stimulation may be untoward in its consequences, and arouses the "fear of crowd" reaction. The stimulating properties of the audience are, among other things, such factors as its size, its remoteness, its familiarity, its interest, its approval, the age, culture, social status, distinction, and authority of its personnel. Small and large doses may arouse different mechanisms, and this fact may explain some of the puzzling aspects of stage fright.

Some drugs are habit-forming; they leave behind them an appetite for more. The same thing is true of the audience in many cases. The lonesome, audience craving retired preacher, of our earlier sections, was an example of this result. McDougall [43] has called attention to this aspect of the desire for an audience, in the following words:

"Admiring response from public gatherings is, as we know, strong drink for any man. Even men long and gradually accustomed to such successes suffer a kind of intoxication on such occasions; and, as with drug, they acquire a morbid need and craving for ever new and larger doses; they cannot live without the limelight.' "

According to the nature of the social situation, the audience arouses emotions, attitudes, and instinctive adjustments and drives, in varying degree and pattern. There is reason indeed for believing that the comparison with the stimulating or disturbing effects of a drug is far from being a mere analogy. Physiological tests show that in many emotional states actual chemical substances are poured out from the internal glands of the body, into the blood stream. It is in part the presence of these chemical agents, in unusual amount, that underlies the dynamogenic influence of excitement, zeal, rage, and of fear.

In direct experiments on the influence of drugs, individual differences in susceptibility are conspicuous. Even in this definite field of physiological reactions so little is known about the causes of these personal differences that they are merely referred to by that vague word "idiosyncrasy." In quite a parallel fashion we must recognize the existence of great personal differences in the nature and degree of the influence of the audience on the individual. The amount of caffein which gives zest and "pep" to the mental activity of one man will throw another into inco-ordination and confusion. Just so, the amount of audience stimulation that brings to one performer an uncommon force and brilliance by arousing his mechanisms of exhibition, will throw another into tremor and dismay through the excitation of fear and the conflict thus introduced.

In common also with most stimulants, the reaction to the audience is toned down by adaptation and experience. In time the dose or situation that formerly produced constraint, interference, and awkwardness comes to yield only a mild exhilaration. Moreover, on the single occasion the initial effects of a stimulant are often most severe, and after the dose recovery sets in and in many cases is complete before the occasion is at an end. In drug experimentation the effects of suggestion,—the thought of taking the drug, the excitement of preparing for it, the expectation of results, are so marked that special techniques such as control doses and control squads must be provided. In this way the effects of suggestion may be separately determined and subtracted from the total effect to exhibit the true drug influence. The suggested effects may often be more striking than those of the drug itself.

In a similar way many speakers and performers find that the audience begins to exert its influence long before it is actually present. The anticipation of the occasion, the preparation to meet it, and, in general, the thought of it, may set up profound mental and organic changes. These may be so considerable that the actual appearance before the audience may bring relief. Perhaps the most comfortable effects of adaptation and experience consist in the elimination of these premonitory symptoms.

A further analogy may be suggested. The drug experimentally administered to an individual affected by this anticipatory excitement may have an effect not entirely similar to that which it would have if taken incidentally, or unwittingly, or under the ordinary routine of life. So also the presence of the audience may influence in different ways the performer who suffers from premonitory symptoms and the one who faces the audience without them.

PRACTICAL CONCLUSIONS

1. Reaction to the audience requires different explanations, according to the individual, the circumstances and the nature of the reaction; three suggestive explanations are suggested, some combination of which is usually required for an actual case.

2. According to one explanation the reaction to the audience is a fear response, in which typical adjustments of flight, aggression, immobility, collapse, and manipulative activity are variously represented.

3. Another explanation suggests that stage fright is a typical conflict neurosis, occasioned by the struggle of two opposed and approximately equal tendencies or instincts—exhibitionism or display on the one hand and fear on the other.

4. Another suggestion is that stage fright represents the re-

arousal, by public appearance, of some humiliation, dread, or feeling of inferiority, such as was formerly experienced in some personal dilemma not itself necessarily connected with appearance before an audience.

5. Among the feasible correctives of audience fear may be suggested (a) adaptation through practice; (b) adoption of the problem attitude rather than the self-attentive attitude or the suggestible attitude; (c) discovery of the original occasion or first cause; (d) re-education or understanding of the mechanism and of the present cue which functions for the old context; and, especially (e) the development, in different circumstances, of more triumphant and confident reactions in connection with audiences and groups.

6. Response to the audience exhibits many of the features characteristic of an intoxication; the debauch of eloquence is no less genuine than that of the drug and may ultimately rest on biochemical processes such as commonly accompany emotional states.

BIBLIOGRAPHY

The following articles or books have been referred to or utilized in preparing the foregoing pages. Reference to these is made by number in the text.

1. Adams, H. F. "The Effect of Climax and Anticlimax Order," *Journal of Applied Psychology*, Dec., 1920.

2. Allport, F. H. "The Influence of the Group upon Association and Thought," *Journal of Experimental Psychology*, June, 1920.

3. Allport, F. H. *Social Psychology*, Houghton Mifflin, Chap. 11. By permission of and by special arrangement with the publishers.

4. Bautain, L. E. *The Art of Extempore Speaking*, p. 261. Scribners, 1839.

5. Benchley, Robert. "Out Front," *Harpers Magazine*, March, 1926.

6. Bentley, M. *A Preface to Social Psychology*, Psychological Review Monographs, Vol. XXI, No. 4, 1916.

7. Brown, W. and Wong, H. "Effects of Surroundings upon Mental Work," *Journal of Comparative Psychology*, August, 1923, pp. 319-326.

8. Buehler, E. C. "The Creation of Atmosphere by the Reader," Master's Essay, Northwestern University, 1923.

9. Burnham, W. H. "The Group as a Stimulus to Mental Activity," *Science*, Vol. XXXI, 1910, pp. 761-767.

10. Burke, E. *Essay on the Sublime and the Beautiful.* 6th Ed., Dodsley, 1770.

11. Burtt, H. E. "The Inspiration-Expiration Rate during Truth and Falsehood," *Journal of Experimental Psychology*, Feb., 1921.

12. Clark, Helen. *The Crowd,* Psychological Review Monographs, Vol. XXI, 1916.

13. Collins, G. R. "The Relative Effectiveness of Condensed and Extended Motive Appeal," *Quarterly Journal of Speech,* Vol. X, 1924, pp. 221-230.

14. Douglass, H. R. *Modern Methods in High School Teaching,* Houghton Mifflin, 1926, p. 207. By permission of and by special arrangement with the publishers.

15. Erickson, C. I. and King, I. "A Comparison of Visual and Oral Presentation," *School and Society,* Vol. 6, 1917.

16. Freeman, F. N., *et al. Visual Instruction,* University of Chicago Press, 1924.

17. Gates, A. I. *Psychology for Students of Education,* Macmillan, 1930.

18. Gates, G. S. An Experimental Study of the Growth of Social Perception, *Journal of Educational Psychology,* Nov., 1923.

19. Gates, G. S. "A Preliminary Study of a Test for Social Perception," *Journal of Educational Psychology,* Oct., 1925.

20. Gates, G. S. "The Effect of an Audience upon Performance," *Journal of Abnormal and Social Psychology,* Jan., 1924.

21. Gates, G. S. and Rissland, L. "The Effect of Encouragement and Discouragement upon Performance," *Journal of Educational Psychology,* Vol. XIV, No. 1, Jan., 1923.

22. Gilchrist, E. P. "The Extent to which Praise and Reproof Affect a Pupil's Work," *School and Society,* Dec. 2, 1916.

23. Goodhue, M. L. *The Cure of Stage Fright,* The Four Seas Co., 1927. By permission of the author.

24. Gray, W. S. *Summary of Investigations Relating to Reading,* Educational Monographs, No. 28, June, 1925, University of Chicago.

25. Griffith, C. R. *General Introduction to Psychology,* Macmillan, 1923. Rev. 1928. By permission.

26. Hollingworth, H. L. *Advertising and Selling,* Appleton, 1913.

27. Hollingworth, H. L. *Abnormal Psychology*, Ronald Press, 1930.
28. Hollingworth, H. L. "The Influence of Alcohol," *Journal of Abnormal and Social Psychology*, Nos. 3 and 4, Oct., 1923, and Jan., 1924.
29. Hollingworth, H. L. and Poffenberger, A. T. *Applied Psychology*, Appleton, 1917, Chap. 8.
30. James, William. *The Principles of Psychology*, Vol. I, pp. 293 ff., Holt, 1890.
31. Jersild, A. T. "Modes of Emphasis in Public Speaking," *Journal of Applied Psychology*, Dec., 1928.
32. Johnson, P. A. "The Permanence of Learning in Elementary Botany," *Journal of Educational Psychology*, Jan., 1930, pp. 37 ff.
33. Jones, H. E. *Experimental Studies of College Teaching*, Archives of Psychology, No. 68, 1923.
34. Judson, L. S. "Objective Studies of the Influence of the Speaker on the Audience," *Journal of Expression*, Vol. IV, March, 1930, pp. 1-11.
35. Kenagy, H. G. and Yoakum, C. S. *Selection and Training of Salesmen*, McGraw-Hill, 1925.
36. Kirkpatrick, E. A. "An Experimental Study of Memory," *Psychological Review*, Vol. I, 1894.
37. Kleiser, G. *How to Speak in Public.* Funk and Wagnalls, 1916.
38. Lacy, J. V. "Relative Value of Motion Pictures as an Educational Agency," *Teachers College Record*, Nov., 1919.
39. Laird, D. A. "Changes in Motor Control, etc., under the Influence of Razzing," *Journal of Experimental Psychology*, June, 1923.
40. LeBon, G. *The Crowd*, Macmillan. By permission.
41. Lippmann, W. *Public Opinion*, Harcourt, Brace and Howe, 1922.
42. Lund, F. H. "The Psychology of Belief," *Journal of Abnormal Psychology*, XX, I, April, 1925.

42A. Marple, C. H. "The Comparative Susceptibility of Three Age Levels to the Suggestion of Group versus Expert Opinion," *Journal of Social Psychology*, 1933, pp. 4, 176-186.

43. McDougall, W. *Social Psychology*, Luce, 1918.

44. McDougall, W. *Outline of Abnormal Psychology*, Scribners, 1926. By permission.

45. McIlvaine. *Elocution*, Scribners, 1870.

46. Millson, W. A. D. "Experimental Work in Audience Reaction," *Quarterly Journal of Speech*, XVIII, Feb., 1932, pp. 13-30.

47. Moore, H. T. "Comparative Influence of Majority and Expert Opinion," *American Journal of Psychology*, Jan., 1921.

48. Moore, H. T. "Laboratory Tests of Anger, Fear, and Sex Interest," *American Journal of Psychology*, July, 1917.

49. Moore, H. T. "The Attention Value of Lecturing without Notes," *Journal of Educational Value*, X, 1919.

50. Moore, T. V. *Image and Meaning in Memory and Perception*, Psychological Review Monographs, No. 27, 1919, p. 281.

51. Morgan, J. J. B. *The Overcoming of Distraction and Other Resistances*, Archives of Psychology, No. 35, 1916.

52. Nixon, H. K. "Popular Answers to Some Psychological Questions," *American Journal of Psychology*, July, 1925.

53. Overstreet, H. A. *Influencing Human Behavior*, Peoples Institute Publishing Co., 1925. By permission of W. W. Norton Company, Inc.

54. Poffenberger, A. T. "Conditions of Belief in Advertising," *Journal of Applied Psychology*, March, 1923.

55. Poffenberger, A. T. *Psychology in Advertising*, Shaw, 1932.

56. Revesz, G. and Hazewinkel, J. F. "The Didactic Value of Lantern Slides and Films," *British Journal of Psychology*, XV, 1924.

57. Rivers, W. H. R. *Instinct and the Unconscious*, Cambridge University Press, 1920.

58. Ruckmick, C. A. *A Preliminary Study of the Emotions*, Psychological Monographs, No. 136, 1921, pp. 30-35.
59. Ruger, H. A. *The Psychology of Efficiency*, Archives of Psychology, No. 15, 1910.
60. Scott, W. D. *The Psychology of Public Speaking*, Pearson, 1907.
61. Stevens, W. E. "A Rating Scale for Public Speakers," *Quarterly Journal of Speech*, XIV, 1928, pp. 223-232.
62. Sumstine, D. R. "Visual Instruction in High School," *School and Society*, Feb. 23, 1918.
63. Tilton, J. W. and Knowlton, D. C. "The Contribution of Ten Chronicles-of-America Photoplays to Seventh Grade History Teaching," *Journal of Social Psychology*, I, 1, Feb., 1930.
64. Travis, L. E. "The Effect of a Small Audience upon Eye-hand Co-ordination," *Journal of Abnormal and Social Psychology*, XX, 1925, pp. 142-146.
65. Trotter, W. *Instincts of the Herd in Peace and War*, Macmillan. By permission.
66. Utterback, W. E. "Measuring the Reaction of the Audience to an Argumentative Speech," *Quarterly Journal of Speech*, VIII, April, 1922, pp. 180-183.
67. Washburne, J. N. "An Experimental Study of Various Graphic, Tabular, and Textual Methods of Presenting Quantitative Materials," *Journal of Educational Psychology*, Sept. and Oct., 1927.
68. Weaver, A. T. "Experimental Studies in Vocal Expression," *Journal of Applied Psychology*, March and June, 1924.
69. Weber, J. "Comparative Effectiveness of Some Visual Aids in Seventh Grade Instruction," *Educational Screen*, 1922, p. 131.
70. Wheeler, R. H. *The Science of Psychology*, Thos. Y. Crowell Co., 1929. By permission.
71. Woodward, H. S. "Measurement and Analysis of Audience Opinion," *Quarterly Journal of Speech*, XIV, 1928, pp. 94-111.

72. Woolbert, C. H. *The Audience*, Psychological Review Monographs, Vol. XXI, 1916.
73. Woolbert, C. H. "The Effects of Various Modes of Public Reading," *Journal of Applied Psychology*, Vol. IV, 1920.
74. Worcester, D. A. "Memory by Visual and Auditory Presentation," *Journal of Educational Psychology*, Jan., 1924.
75. Yerkes, R. M. and Yoakum, C. S. *Army Mental Tests*, Holt, 1920.